Success Is A Side Effect:
Leadership, Relationships, and Selective Amnesia

MONICA F. ANDERSON

BOOKS BY THIS AUTHOR

Black English Vernacular: From Ain't to Yo' Mama
Mom, Are We There Yet?
When a Sistah's Fed Up
I Stand Accused
Sinphony

Visit Monica "Dr. mOe" Anderson's website at
www.drmOeanderson.com
Twitter/@drmOeanderson
iTunes Podcasts/Dr. mOe Anderson
YouTube/drmoeutube

Praise for Success is a Side Effect

Dr. "mOe" synthesized her years of experience as a professional, family woman, and community leader into *Success Is a Side Effect*, a no-nonsense guide to navigating the pitfalls, challenges, and triumphs on your march to the executive suite. As you read through real-life problems and solutions, you get a master class in corporate ascension from a trusted mentor…delivered with humor and candor. These are insights your manager won't tell you and your mother may not know. Whether you need help getting to the next rung on the ladder of success or can't seem to make sense of your personal life, it's time to find out why success is truly a side effect.
Anne Boyd, Writer | Editor | Critic
www.anneabouttown.com

....

This book is an instructional compendium of knowledge. Dr. Anderson weaves advice, compassion, allegory, and scenarios in each and every lesson. Readers will be able to utilize this "roadmap to self-improvement" like a GPS reference guide to actually plan the improvements, as they progress through the curriculum. What a priceless "gift"!
Marilyn D. Johnson
Global Ambassador/Speaker | Retired IBM Corporate Executive |
Wilhemina Model
www.marilynjspeaks.com

This is a must-read for the busy professional seeking coaching with humor. Dr. mOe weaves a tale of success to help already accomplished people do even better. I loved it!
Sheryl Cole, JD
Mayor Pro Tem, City of Austin, TX

Very inspiring! This book is a must-read for every woman looking to get ahead in business. I especially liked the bullet points and discussion questions. They make it easy to review the important points and form a personal plan of action. As a professional who has advised clients on wealth strategies for over two decades, I know Dr. Anderson's sound, practical tips will put you on the path to financial independence.
Becky L. Walker, CFP®
President, Wealth Strategies, Inc.
www.wealthstrategiesinc.us

We make choices every day. Moe's book does an excellent job of speaking to your inner voice. She encourages you to get out of your own way. I've accomplished a lot in my lifetime, but I needed a dose of energy and a reminder that I should do more things that scare me. Moe's book speaks to the inner do-gooder in me. It also makes me want to hug myself a little more. Every young professional should read this book.
Terri B. Williams
Vice President-Government Relations |
American Heart Association-SW Affiliate

Dr. Monica Anderson's book is a great read for aspiring and established professional women alike. Her tenets of success are practical and outline best practices for women looking to climb the corporate ladder, rise in rank, or start a successful enterprise. *Success Is a Side Effect* is a go-to book when you need guidance and reference on how to be the successful woman you were destined to be.
Natalie Madeira Cofield
Founder, Walker's Legacy
President & CEO, Greater Austin Black Chamber of Commerce.

I found *Success Is a Side Effect* to be a great read for women of all ages and all careers. Since change, and often the transitions we experience as a result of change, continue to be affected by one's choices, this book helps one reevaluate the thought process for making choices, commends one for the choices one has made, and offers one the security of making a change at any point in one's life.
Marie "Doc" Holliday, DMD
Dentist | Entrepreneur
www.dochollidayfw.com

All readers will find much to stimulate their thinking in this book about pursuing excellence and being a leader in every role, whether you are in the classroom or the boardroom. The use of personal anecdotes, research, statistics, and humor to illustrate life management strategies is brilliant. As I continue to inspire girls and women to be PHENOMENAL, this book will serve as a guide to success not just for them but also for myself.
Rashaanne N. Lewis
Founder/President & CEO, Girls Inc. of Greater Austin

....

Moe writes with sincere passion and clarity, which makes this book a go-to manual for busy professionals who want to get ahead. Her insights guide you to make the best decisions for your career and life. The coaching she provides short-circuits common mistakes and puts you on a path to certainty and success. I highly recommend it!

Shuronda Robinson
President/CEO Adisa Communications
www.makingthingsclear.com

Success Is A Side Effect:
Leadership, Relationships, and Selective Amnesia

MONICA F. ANDERSON

Austin, Texas

Success Is a Side Effect: Leadership, Relationships, and Selective Amnesia

For information, business or promotional use, or quantity discounts, please e-mail info@drmoeanderson.com or write to:

TyMAC Books
Special Sales Department
P.O. Box 150484
Austin, Texas 78715

Business/Personal Growth/Leadership/Success/Life Management

Cover photo: Dwayne Hills
Cover and Interior design: CreateSpace

Table of Contents

CONTENTS

Dedication

*This book is for all the people who taught me
that the best leaders are even better team players.*

Foreword

Be warned: you may not "like" this book.

Here's why.

Dr. mOe Anderson tells the truth.

And truth can be uncomfortable.

In your face.

Needed.

You may not "like" this book.

But you just might "need" it.

I know I did.

I am a successful woman of power.

We all are.

Even if we use that power to keep our lives in turmoil, we are still powerful.

But are we human?

Do you and I give ourselves the internal permission to cry, or curse, or call a spade a spade?

Do we take responsibility for handicapping our loved ones so we feel needed?

Do we rob our bodies of much-needed rest so we can finish the job?

If you are anything like me, you have made it by pushing through, making it happen, and, on some very real and tangible levels, self-sacrificing.

But, are you happy?

Are you free?

Can you stand up for yourself without talking down to others?

Are you willing to put distance between yourself and people who diminish you?

These are the "truth" questions Dr. mOe indirectly pushes you to examine.

Here, she shoots from the hip.

She ignites truth with power—and you may not like it.

But you need it.

I know I did.

I needed a woman to care enough about me to sit down and write out the practical wisdom that most successful women overlook in our drive to be "somebody."

I needed a woman to tell me how others are always watching and that perhaps in my need for approval I am giving them the exact tool they need to cut me off at the knees.

I needed a woman to open her heart about her own body betraying her…feeling like time was a gun pressed against the back of her head, threatening in a hushed whisper, "I can end your life any moment now."

Dr. mOe is a woman who knows that life is literally one breath at a time—and she writes like this pen, this paper, this pad is possibly her last word.

So she's not pulling punches.

She's not sugarcoating.

She is on a mission. She wants her experiences, good and bad, to help others.

Women.

Me.

You.

Us.

In these pages she will make you laugh, look deeply into your humanity, and love yourself better in all of your perfect imperfections.

As I said before: you may not like this book.

But if you are willing to own your power and experience life as sacred breath, you may love this book—and yourself a little more because you read it.

I am of the opinion when a book falls into my life, I have called it to me because my heart, mind, soul, and spirit are ready for me to evolve.

Dr. mOe believes reading and investing in yourself will get you multiple streams of happiness.

I invite you to enjoy this investment of time and intimate self-reflection so you can, with a bit more ease and confidence, be guided more fully to your destiny.

But be warned: this book—which you may not like, but quietly need—can change your life…

Dr. Venus Opal Reese

Defy Impossible Expert &

Million Dollar Moneymaker Strategist™

www.DefyImpossible.com

Introduction

ARE YOU ENOUGH?

Are you kind enough? Assertive enough? Pretty enough? Accomplished enough? Many women struggle with these questions every day. Ultimately, we are wondering if we have a meaningful existence, whether there is a point to the endless challenges in our personal and professional lives. We are encouraged to do "whatever it takes" to become a success. But what exactly does that mean? What is success?

Perhaps you're recalling the accomplishments of elite female leaders in corporate America such as Shonda Rhimes, executive producer, Sheryl Sandberg, CEO of Facebook, or Sara Blakely, founder and CEO of Spanx as examples of genuine change agents. If so, I challenge that restrictive "short list" and encourage you to reexamine your definition of success. Women currently hold about 4 percent of the Fortune 500 CEO positions. If only women in comparable positions define success, then 96 percent of us are unsuccessful, or we simply possess incalculable influence that doesn't make headlines 96 percent of the time.

We matter.

Powerful female leaders are everywhere: running small businesses, fundraising for nonprofit organizations, inventing, competing, and raising families. The same strategies used for success, such as networking and managing human resources, are necessary to turn effort into positive outcomes regardless of one's title. Likewise, the same emotions, like disappointment and anxiety, accompany a bad assessment from your manager or your mother-in-law. Consider the fact that it costs up to a quarter of a million dollars to raise a child in the United States! If you have four children, that is potentially a million-dollar investment. It takes a fiscally responsible leader to manage financial resources and keep a budget balanced anywhere.

This book is for all the unheralded leaders who must survive, and even thrive, in a world where Cinderella's feet hurt and Sleeping Beauty gets fired for frequent tardiness. What I know for sure is that the women whom the world admires for their inner beauty, confidence, and competence were not born that way; *they were forged.* And in the process, they changed the lives of everyone around them.

We all have the potential, the duty, and the power to lead in our chosen fields. And, ultimately, the choices we make at each intersection of our personal journey, not the title on a business card, determine whether or not we are successful.

I know about going through the fire. There was nothing in the opening pages of my biography to indicate I would become anything other than a soft-spoken scientist. For thirteen years, I was the nerdy only child of two educators until my only sibling was born. When I wasn't glued to my mother's side, I read encyclopedias and played with chemistry sets for fun. My parents punished me by making me go outside and play with the other kids! Now, in my fifth decade of life, I look back in awe at the roads I've traveled. While I love the current destination, the trip would have been so much easier if, decades ago, someone had given me the proven, practical tips I share in this book. Today, I'm a grandmother, a member of management at a national company, a journalist, a multipublished author, a real estate investor, a serial entrepreneur, and a motivational speaker. I feel very good about these accomplishments. I also lost money investing in a can't-miss restaurant venture, was divorced after seventeen years of marriage, struggled through a crippling episode of depression, and parted ways with dear friends a few times. Those difficult experiences temporarily shattered my spirit.

And just when I thought I'd been through hell and survived, in 2012, I was diagnosed with intestinal cancer. Ironically, cancer used to be my greatest fear. Since my diagnosis, I have generally avoided using the word *survivor* to refer to myself because I thought it meant you are free from disease. As this rare type of sarcoma (GIST) is treatable but has no cure, I didn't feel like a survivor. Then, one day, I was inexplicably moved to look up the definition of *survivor.*

Survivor means to continue to live; a person alive after an event in which others have died; to exist.

It does not mean you are healed, rescued, or no longer facing challenges, nor that you won't die eventually. It means—right now—I'm alive. And I will make the best of *this* day and *this* place and *this* opportunity to be a light despite my own battle with darkness. So I am a survivor, and so are you.

I've spent the past two decades writing, speaking, and coaching others on survival tactics for business and personal relationships.

As recurring themes began to emerge from the challenges my clients faced, I became inspired to pen a book of self-improvement and empowerment strategies for women. It took five years, multiple rewrites, and two keyboards to complete this project. I believe the lessons I've compiled in this book can be helpful to women at any stage of their personal development. These proven, practical principles are given without a lot of complicated jargon or examples that only apply to the elite 4 percent. My only goal is to help you ramp up your *career* and strengthen your personal relationships because, in short, success is a feeling, not a destination, and everyone should experience it.

The take-away from these life lessons, in fact, from every life lesson, is that success is the side effect of making better choices every day.

Lesson One:
Prescription for Happiness

THE FOLLOWING CHAPTERS expand on ten strategies that appear easy to implement in isolation, but can be very difficult to execute simultaneously. Most likely, you are doing great at five or six of these strategies, okay at three, and you suck at two. I put this list up front so you can revisit it at least twice a year and assess where you are experiencing challenges. Balance these rules, and a balanced, happier life is sure to follow.

1. **Pursue your passions, not people.** Independent women have inner beauty and outer charisma that can't be purchased at a boutique or cosmetics counter.

2. Avoid the fear factor. Every great endeavor has great risks. **When you fall, fall forward.** Learn from your mistakes in life and love. Then, try again, more intelligently.

3. Delegate. Success demands your single focus. **You can't achieve great outcomes with mediocre effort.** We mock men for not being able to multitask—watch the baby,

cook, wash, and plan a vacation while changing a light bulb—yet the majority of Fortune 500 CEOs are men. Obviously, it is not a handicap to do one thing at a time.

4. **Don't quit!** Your life is a delicate soufflé, not microwave popcorn. It takes time and effort to reach realistic goals. Author Malcolm Gladwell says it takes ten thousand hours to become an expert at a "cognitively demanding activity." That's 1,250 eight-hour days of practice. Don't give up too soon on school, your new role at work, or learning a new skill.

5. Never roar like a lion. You don't have to be one of the boys to compete in co-ed sports, politics, or the work place. **Effectively communicate without screaming** and you'll be respected (and heard).

6. **Embrace your place.** Have a few friends your own age. The glamour mags are lying. Forty is not the new thirty, and twenty is not the new fifty. Do not waste precious moments in the present with mourning or envy of the past.

7. Change your mind often. Change is part of growth, and stubborn pride is worthless in the store of life. **Try new things and test new ideas.** "You haven't changed a bit in twenty years" is not a compliment. You should be better than you were twenty years ago.

8. Eat lunch with strangers. Plants follow the same sun every day. You are not a plant. **Spend time conversing with people in other age groups, of other ethnicities, and of the opposite gender** if you truly strive to reach new heights. Avoid cliques and broaden your knowledge of human nature by broadening your network.

9. **Schedule your mental breakdowns.** Why randomly fall apart when you can take a vacation, take a nap, or retreat to the bathroom for ten minutes and relax your mind? Refreshed bodies are more creative and productive.

10. **Never close your heart unless it's temporarily under reconstruction.** Loving your neighbor as yourself is not optional. This is a mandate, not a suggestion.

Lesson Two: Be Fierce

WISE AND FEARLESS leaders take counsel from everyone. The cook and the immediate past president both have valuable life experiences that can strengthen the foundation of your success. However, they may also have an axe to grind, so wise leaders follow the number one rule of survival—Keep Some Secrets! Being cautious and seeking life-balance are not mutually exclusive, so it's important to delegate or discreetly "Dial 911" to a loyal, trustworthy friend *before* you become overwhelmed. And, even fearless leaders may selectively exhibit vulnerability. Displaying soft character traits, such as humility and compassion, deter the animosity of the insecure.

ATTITUDE CHECKUP

Women who display any emotion are usually portrayed as whiny or bitchy. It doesn't matter if they have a legitimate right to be whiny bitches; no one hears the content, just the tone. Successful leaders often adopt a poker face, a poker voice, and a poker body. What does that mean? It means that when they speak, they control the tone of their voice, the pace of their words, and the content of their remarks so that it is difficult to gauge what they are thinking. This gives them a distinct advantage in the high-stakes politics of the workplace because others cannot easily manipulate their reactions. It makes them appear more powerful and superior to ordinary people. Admittedly, acquiring these skills takes patience and practice, but it is well worth the effort.

These are survival skills every savvy politician has mastered. Watch the debates and interviews during any election year. The candidates remain calm in the face of protestors, hecklers, vicious personal attacks, and defeat. These people are human. You know that they are hurt and angered, yet they rarely, if ever, display these emotions.

In the bestseller *The Forty-Eight Laws of Power,* Robert Greene asserts, "An emotional response to a situation is the single greatest barrier to power, a mistake that will cost you a lot more than any temporary satisfaction you might gain by expressing your feelings. Emotions cloud reason, and if you cannot see the situation clearly, you cannot prepare and respond to it with any degree of control."

All of us know at least one drama queen or drama king. These people love to yell and make a scene when they're offended. While all of that screaming might make them feel better in the short term, in the long term it does nothing for their careers or their relationships. Seriously, how often can you give someone a piece of your mind before you run out of brain?

....

Screaming says more about you than the person you are attacking.

....

However, showing no emotion is not the same as feeling no emotion. Don't close your heart unless it's temporarily under reconstruction. Selfishness, cynicism, and sarcasm are also negative displays of emotion. Additionally, they are symptoms of a more serious disorder anthropologist Ashley Montague termed "psychosclerosis" or hardening of the attitude. Physicians prescribe medication for arteriosclerosis, also known as hardening of the arteries. Left untreated, arteriosclerosis may lead to physical death. It's equally important for you to rid yourself of psychosclerosis because it inhibits your ability to think strategically, which may result in your professional death. You must use your emotional intelligence: that gut feeling that tells you when to appear maternal and when to appear majestic. The important thing is to act with more purpose than passion.

Former Secretary of State Condoleeza Rice, is a perfect example of grace under pressure. She was accused of everything from not being black enough (whatever that means) to having an illicit love affair with the 43rd President of the United States of America. These are harsh allegations against a very accomplished, intelligent woman. It is conceivable that these rumors hurt her feelings. Our natural reaction when we're hurt is to lash out at our critics. As the saying goes, "hurt people, hurt people." Yet, Secretary Rice never publicly lost her temper refuting these claims. In fact, she barely addressed them. She kept her focus on her goal of doing the best job she could as a member of the president's cabinet. When the rumors die their natural death, you will be remembered for what you accomplished, not what others said about you.

The workplace relationship is like any other relationship you may have, whether as a parent, girlfriend, or wife. You must constantly assess the situation you're facing and decide the appropriate action for that moment. It may be a pat on the back. It may be a kick in the butt. It must always be in the best interest of everyone you value, including...no, especially, YOU.

KEEP SOME SECRETS

The greatest assets you own are your ideas. You must protect your priceless intellectual property at all times. Seek counsel, take good advice, but *keep some secrets* (especially at work.) Like church, work is not a building; it's the role you play among the people accompanying you. The surroundings don't matter. If you're with a colleague, a potential colleague, or a former colleague, you are working. It's unimportant whether you're in a boardroom, at happy hour, at the company picnic, or at the conference hotel's indoor pool; never let your guard down. Don't drink too much or say anything you don't want broadcast on the world news, Tweeted, or posted. Even better, imagine you're on Ustream live video 24/7, and all the world is watching. Govern yourself accordingly. Telling the truth does not mean telling everything you know.

Be assured, someone wants your position or simply doesn't want you to have it. I don't know why. Some people are crazy. They lie awake nights imagining ways to sabotage you... just because. As working women, we are constantly competing, and America loves winners. Win-win (as in I benefit and you benefit, so everyone is happy) sounds sweet, and it's great for customer service, but not for keeping your job, keeping your partner, or growing your business.

True, you cannot operate in a vacuum. You must interact with others in order to plan, collaborate on projects, and try to take over the world, or, at least, the bowling league brackets. Just be very selective about when and where you share your best ideas and resources. Don't brainstorm about your invention with everyone at bingo or save your revolutionary process on a shared computer, even in an "invisible" file. Don't leave important documents on or in your unlocked desk. Don't share your personal finance issues. Don't talk about your relationships or your marriage in a way that exposes the challenges you face or the good fortune your family experiences. Don't give your password to anyone at the office, including your BFF. Human resource professionals frown on that practice, and there are few feelings worse than having a friend slowly turn on you like a Ferris wheel at the state fair.

....
The greatest assets you own are your ideas.
....

Share what you must to ensure everyone's success because that is team play at its finest, and we all benefit from consistent contribution to process improvements. But never divulge more to your peers than you receive until they have proven they can be trusted. It's important to notice if they never share important ideas/information with you without prompting. Do they always seem to wait until after you've gotten the information from another source to fill in the blanks with their superior knowledge of the situation? Why didn't they share before? Hmmmm? Is that a pattern?

Of course, this principle doesn't apply to your boss or partner. Never, ever surprise your boss, except when you are under budget and ahead of schedule. In fact, once or twice a month, send a brief update to your boss on the positive progress of you and your team members. Do the same thing at home, too. Keep the most important people in your life well-informed about what you are doing and why.

Use your instinct, experience, and office gossip to determine who is the least trustworthy among your acquaintances. Don't supply gossip; just listen to it. Pay close attention to the person who attributes every negative comment to someone else. This person is baiting you to say something he or she can repeat as well. Watch everyone's behavior. People who steal time by clocking in late or leaving early every day will steal your ideas. Minutes are money. They are stealing from the employer and they might steal from you as well.

This strategy is also applicable to dealing with technicians, salespeople, and others with whom you negotiate, especially males. Have you ever noticed how good men are at answering only the part(s) of your question they feel like addressing? For example, in the middle of writing this book, I realized that someone with whom I contracted to do a job had not followed up as promised. This is the verbatim text exchange with that party:

12:04 p.m. (Dr. mOe) "I've inquired about when you can meet in person with my business partner and me twice. You have not responded; it seems difficult to reach you. Do you have another job?"

1:46 p.m. (Response) "Where are you trying to reach me? This number or e-mail is best."

Notice he did not say that he didn't get my previous communications. He did not apologize for not responding to them. He did not apologize for taking almost two hours to respond to my text, allegedly "the best" way to reach him. Most women would have gone to great lengths to explain to me why they didn't respond sooner. The man simply ignored the question, possibly because he was busy on his other job or (more likely) he didn't feel the need to divulge that information.

Do not assume that people didn't hear you, didn't read all of your e-mail bullets, or didn't understand you. Maybe they are just keeping secrets of their own. Instead of becoming frustrated and repeating yourself over and over, recognize this type of communication as an intentional action to keep you off balance. My response to him—the following day—was a simple "Okay. Thanks." He called a few minutes later, and he has been much more responsive to me since he correctly translated that terse response as "You are about to lose a client." Sometimes less really is more.

This sounds harsh, but reality is harsh. The minute you forget this critical principle, you invite a power struggle. Even the legendary Queen of Egypt, Cleopatra VII, known equally for her guile and beauty, was betrayed by her baby brother and forced into exile. Her alliance with Julius Caesar (and others) restored her status. Now, this is a historic lesson in strategic partnerships. The lesson: love thy neighbor but watch your purse.

CALL 911

If you want that R-E-S-P-E-C-T that Aretha Franklin croons about, learn to D-E-L-E-G-A-T-E. The only thing worse than someone who thinks she knows everything is someone who thinks she can do everything. Humans have different skills, titles, and temperaments for a reason. Your team may be as small as a supportive partner or a loving parent or it may be as large as Martha Stewart's enterprise, but it's rare that anyone does anything spectacular without any help.

Great endeavors require a focused leader. It is hard to focus on the big picture and attend to every detail. Allow others to help you. Let your assistants assist. Make your accountant accountable. Give the people supporting you an opportunity to think and work at *your* pace, but with their *own* rhythm. Students get "progress reports" to take home every six weeks or so. Teachers don't call parents after every quiz or daily grade with an update. Imagine how distracting that would become.

Yet, some people are constantly badgering the people on their team about their progress on a project and then complaining about their lack of progress. Or they have nine million fruitless meetings to talk about what hasn't been done. Try allowing the people who work around or under you to give you scheduled updates versus constantly having to report every action or clear every decision with you. That is too time consuming for both of you, and it indicates an obsession with exerting control...or a poor hiring decision.

Different people require different levels of supervision. New employees naturally need more instruction than someone who has been with your company for many years. However, everyone must reach the point, eventually, where you don't need to direct their actions like an air traffic controller, or they should be grounded for good. If your home or business falls apart every time you are away, that means you are a poor leader, not a good one. Good leaders, like good parents, prepare others to operate independently. I'm not suggesting things aren't better when you're around, but I am saying it shouldn't be a hot mess when you get back.

....
You can do it all, but you can't do it all well.
Learn to delegate.
....

In dentistry, staff members require "direct" or "indirect" supervision. Dental hygienists, who have two years or more of advanced education after high school, can legally provide treatment on a patient without the dentist being present in the operatory. This is an example of indirect supervision. Because hygienists actually produce income for a dental practice while the dentist is busy in another operatory, they are very valuable to a practice. Some hygienists make almost as much as a recently licensed dentist! Your goal, as you expand your personal empire, must be to employ people who produce income for your enterprise whether you are present or not. Micromanaging takes your energy away from growth and places it on maintenance.

Don't *do* the small stuff if you can find a competent person to do it. A wise woman with a growing business or family realizes that she is not the only one who can answer the phone and pay bills. She searches for a capable assistant until she finds just the right person, or she will be forever limited to the number of hours she can go without sleep.

Delegating at home is as important as delegating at the office. If we want our sons and daughters, our younger brothers and sisters, or our acquaintances to have balanced lives that include work, rest, and play, then we need to role-model that balance. If your actions say you can do everything at anytime without any help, don't complain when everyone is happy to let you be Batwoman and save the world. Why doesn't Batwoman have a sidekick anyway, like Batman, Robinson Crusoe, and the Lone Ranger? And why is she wearing a swimsuit and boots? What kind of crime-fighting attire is that? Superman wore flats and Batman had a butler. Batwoman is fictional. That's why. Keep it real.

....

You can do it all but you cannot do it all well.
Someone or something will suffer.

....

We know kids don't arrive in the delivery room lazy and spoiled. Selfish, yes, but not lazy. The common conception is that we manufacture lazy children. Too often, women (and men) benignly spoil their sons and daughters. Have you made a conscious effort to train your child/grandchild/mentee to be responsible and compassionate? Does he or she know how to cook, clean, and wash? Can your daughter shop for groceries on a budget, balance a checkbook, and get her tires rotated every five thousand miles? Are you teaching your children life skills that will sustain them, with or without a partner?

If not, why not? Doing everything for them or paying someone to do everything for them is not a gift. It's a handicap. The result is lazy men whose wives resent the mothers-in-law they blame for their husbands' behavior and lazy women who can't handle adversity.

Don't set youths up for failure in future relationships because they believe one person is supposed to do all the work, like their "mom" did for them. In the words of Phyllis Diller, "Housework won't kill you, but why take the chance?"

Delegate fairly and regularly. Everyone benefits.

CRY A LITTLE

Remember the commercial admonishing, "Never let 'em see you sweat"? Actually, it's okay to let them see you sweat—a little. Selectively showing a lack of strength is not the same as revealing your weaknesses. Occasionally admitting you are not as perfect as you might seem is endearing to people. It makes you seem human. It often turns (some of) your critics into supporters, especially if you allow them to give you advice for improvement.

When we hear successful people like Nicole Kidman, an Academy Award and Golden Globe winning actress, admit she becomes extremely nervous during public appearances, or hear *American Idol* winner Fantasia say she struggled to put food on the table as a single mother, don't we feel a little less envious about their success? Don't we think, "Great, girlfriend. You did it. You're due some joy." What about Halle Berry's and Julia Roberts's enduring, very expensive, and very public divorces before they found true love? Even divas have relationship troubles. Then, they found new guys and started families. Yay! Right? We were happy for them because we can all relate to man troubles. We don't all have flawless skin and perfect teeth, but relationship issues are universal.

Tell your colleagues that you're bad at math, you have a horrible sense of direction, you're not analytical, your kid made a D in preschool. Ask them for assistance, directions, or parenting advice. Actively listen to their response and receive it enthusiastically. Ask your coworkers probing questions and follow up with a report on your success later. Thank them. I repeat. ***Thank them*** enthusiastically. Gratitude is becoming as scarce as phone booths. Try something like, "Jean, thanks for telling me about that learning program. My son and I spend thirty minutes on it each night and he's already raised his grade to a C. You're a lifesaver!"

Roosters don't crow all day and neither should you. Nobody wants to hear that. It is annoying. So is smiling constantly. Nobody is that happy. If you are, pretend to have a few problems like the rest of us now and then.

I wrote a lifestyle column for a major daily newspaper for several years. I became an "accidental journalist" when one of my Junior League friends shared my writing skills with the editor of the *Arlington Star-Telegram*. I started out as a guest columnist for that bureau (their first African-American columnist) and honed my craft by sharing personal stories about my family, with the caveat, of course, that I kept some things secret. Most of my articles were humorous, but my favorite editor, Ashley, taught me "that which is most painful is most universal." He was right. In 2000, the executive editor of the *Fort-Worth Star Telegram*, Jim Witt, asked me to become a regular Sunday Life columnist for all the editions. That's a coveted spot at any newspaper and a major undertaking, considering I was a mother of two in full-time private practice at that time.

I've always loved writing, but what had the greatest impact on my paid career as both a writer and a speaker was my choice to join the Junior League, a nonprofit service organization, and write for their community magazine for no pay! The columns I wrote about my maternal grandmother dying and my divorce, a few years later, got twenty times more voice mails and letters from readers than my usual subjects about raising a family and the challenges of being a working mom. I'll never forget all I learned from those experiences and those choices. Today, I continue to cry a little and share topics that are universal.

Importantly, when trying to decide what to share and what not to share about your life, whether on Facebook, on LinkedIn, or over coffee, ask yourself two questions:

1. Is this something most people can relate to?

2. Could this negatively affect my reputation now or in the future?

If the answers are yes and no, go ahead and share. If the answers are yes and yes, proceed with caution. For example, someone going through a bitter divorce is joining the ranks of 50 percent of first-time married couples. Most people can relate to it. However, someone going through a long, difficult divorce is often consumed by the process to the point of losing her inner filter. Discussing intimate details of personal finances or allegations of infidelity with anyone who will listen may damage your reputation just as much as your soon-to-be ex's. The rival who wants your position will happily bring up your difficult situation every time you miss work for a court appearance or turn in less than stellar work.

Perhaps you're a graduate student who goes on drinking binges. Most people have been exposed to someone who drinks heavily.

But what if you've applied for a fellowship and the competition is stiff? Unlike the real housewives of wherever, you need to rehab privately.

I'm not trying to confuse you. Keep some things to yourself. Just don't keep everything to yourself. Don't be that weird chick who always eats lunch alone in her car and never talks about her vacation. Volunteer the fact that you got sunburned while on vacation. Talk about the cute cabana boy who made you a virgin Sex on the Beach cocktail, but do not chat about how you got sloppy drunk and made out with him on the beach.

You gotta give 'em something. Otherwise, folks will speculate about what's wrong with you. Yes, there is something wrong with you, and if you think there isn't, life or your relatives will eventually persuade you to reconsider.

Dahlin', if you feed the piranhas, they are less likely to attack you.

LESSON TWO SUMMARY

☞ Public displays of anger diminish your power.

☞ No matter where you are, if colleagues are present—you're working. Govern yourself accordingly.

☞ Listen to office gossip but don't repeat it.

☞ Guard against "psychosclerosis" or hardening of the attitude.

☞ Learn to delegate at work and at home.

☞ Don't share every detail of your personal life. It can and will be used against you.

☞ Selectively reveal your "softer" side.

Lesson Three:
Food, Water, Romance

BEYONCÉ IS A top-grossing entertainer, as well as an actress, producer, model, and businesswoman. She is truly amazing, but the world does not need another Beyoncé or Erika Leonard, aka E. L. James, author of the *Fifty Shades of Grey* trilogy. To stand out from the crowd you must create, not recreate. From hipster to hip replacement, always strive for originality, ingenuity, and high self-esteem. Learn from others, but don't try to become them. Individual success derives from the unique gifts, talents, skills, and personality each person possesses. It is a mistake that time cannot erase to be anything less than authentic.

WHAT A GIRL NEEDS

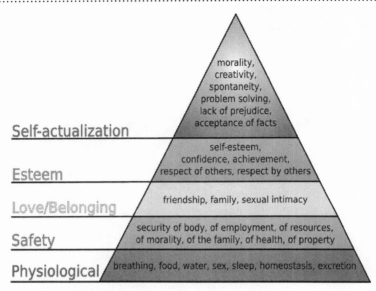

Self-actualization

morality, creativity, spontaneity, problem solving, lack of prejudice, acceptance of facts

Esteem

self-esteem, confidence, achievement, respect of others, respect by others

Love/Belonging

friendship, family, sexual intimacy

Safety

security of body, of employment, of resources, of morality, of the family, of health, of property

Physiological

breathing, food, water, sex, sleep, homeostasis, excretion

MASLOW'S HIERARCHY OF NEEDS. (HTTP://EN.WIKIPEDIA.ORG/WIKI/
IMAGE:MASLOW%27S_HIERARCHY_OF_NEEDS.SVG) /© 2006 J. FINKELSTEIN,/
WIKIMEDIA COMMONS/GNU FREE DOCUMENTATION LICENSE 1.2

This illustration represents psychologist Abraham Maslow's renowned, seventy-year-old theory on the hierarchy of needs. It starts at the foundation with basic needs such as air, rest, sex, and water, all of which are mandatory to sustain life. Sex as a basic need is debatable, but affection or romance may be substituted for sex, in my opinion. The apex of the pyramid is self-actualization, or becoming your personal best by exploring your creative capacity without the constraints of bias and feelings of inferiority. Greatly simplified, Maslow's theory was that the first four levels must be met before you can reach the highest level. Level one is a no-brainer. A deficit of air, food, or water results in death. None of us should be surprised by level two, where we see the need for safety, structure, and stability. Even a child wants these things. Nor would most of us disagree with the third level, love and belonging. The most successful career can seem empty without the concurrent joys of intimacy, affection, and friends. The critical level in this pyramid, for any woman, is level four: *esteem.* Self-esteem, self-respect, and self-love precede self-actualization.

Maslow later revised this pyramid and added levels, but this original pyramid is still the standard-bearer. If you feel discouraged, inferior, and ineffective, you cannot propel yourself to the boundaries of your destiny. Many of us become derailed at this level because of the self-destructive tendency to compare ourselves to other women whom we believe are superior to us, such as megastar Beyoncé Knowles.

YOU AIN'T BEYONCÉ

Beyoncé is awesome, but girlfriend, you ain't Beyoncé and you don't need to be. Media images, stereotypes, and backstabbing haters constantly reinforce the idea that we will never be thin enough, pretty enough, or smart enough to deserve respect.

Well, they're wrong.

So, you're not part of a think tank or corporate executive Cathie Black, or your perfect cousin who cured her kid's asthma with Vicks VapoRub. That's fine. They have their own destinies. They're doing what they were created to do. Your mission must always be to make the most of your talents. If you suck at addition and subtraction, you will never be dean of the math department at the local university. But, learn to use the Excel program on your computer, and you can still get that spreadsheet done and turned in on time. Quit worrying about what you can't do or can't be. Do you. Do the best, most incredible and phenomenal you imaginable.

....

Originality, not imitation, is the seed
of a bountiful life harvest.

....

Look at your life as it is and as you want it to be. What is stopping you from maximizing your potential? Is it possible those lower level, instinctual, powerful needs have not been met? If so, go back and attempt to fill in the blanks. You can reach great heights on the ladder to success without meeting all these needs, but you'll never know if it's your full potential, just as a world-class sprinter who smokes a pack of cigarettes a day will never know if she might be even faster without the negative effects of tobacco.

I suggest you "do the Maslow." First, take care of your body. Without good health, you can't do anything. Doggedly pursue the education, job, or business opportunity that will allow you to live in a safe, stable environment; don't harbor negativity. Make amends with your cousin, or, at least, extend the olive branch. Just don't loan her money again. Accept the fact that she never pays you back. Find someone special to love, meaning a closer than colleague relationship; someone you can confide in and ask for advice. Lastly, quit comparing yourself to airbrushed cover models. They don't really look like those retouched photos, and they have to be hungry. Remember, food is a basic need! Your only competition is the woman in your mirror...yesterday. Are you better than that woman *today?*

Be good to yourself, and increased confidence will naturally follow. It's a logical progression. After that, the Milky Way is the limit, and, from your new galactic heights, even the pyramids will seem small.

AVOID THE FEAR FACTOR

When talking to young people about goal setting, I often use an illustration taken from Lewis Carroll's famous book, *Alice's Adventures in Wonderland*. You may recall that there is a point where poor Alice is lost in the forest. Her new environment perplexes and frightens her. In the story, Alice asks the Cheshire cat, "Would you tell me, please, which way I ought to go from here?"

He responds, "That depends a good deal on where you want to get to."

Young Alice whispers timidly, "I don't much care where."

To which the cat replies, "Then, it doesn't much matter which way you go."

It does matter which way you go, and the easy way is often not the best way. Before you proceed in a bold, new direction, you must have a plan. Successful women have a plan for every area of their lives from their health, to their careers, to their very souls. You should know what you want to accomplish each day, each week, each month, and each year. You can modify the plan, but you must have a specific goal in mind or you will always feel lost and anxious.

Sometimes the difference between success and failure is not whom you know or what you know; it is simply what you fear. Millions of women are treading deep water in a pool of their melted dreams. No, it is not friends or family stopping most people from reaching their full potential; it is their fear of failure.

The mental transformation required to overcome fear is achieved by focusing on what you will gain, not what you might lose. Fear magnifies the consequences of failure. Some people won't speak in public because they fear people will laugh at them, whisper while they're talking, or fall asleep. Maybe they will. Some people won't ask for help when they desperately need assistance with a project because the person they ask might say no and then send out an inter-office memo telling everyone they're incompetent. That's possible, but unlikely. Fear always exaggerates our concerns if we allow it.

....

Fear magnifies the consequences of failure.

....

Am I advising you to be intrepid: without fear? No, I'm saying take fear in a healthy dose, or as my shero news anchor and cancer survivor, Robin Roberts, says, "When fear knocks, let faith answer." An emergency exit or Plan B should accompany even great faith because wise women prepare for adverse results. Too much fear paralyzes you into having no plan at all, A or B.

Successful people dwell on the possibilities, while others stubbornly obsess over the uncertainties of life. If you want to be better, you have to do more, and that means being uncomfortable not a little bit, not some, but most of the time. That means taking risks. That means doing many boring, horrid, difficult things you don't really want to do, and doing them well. Yes, you will make mistakes. Don't become preoccupied with your failures. Learn the lessons of your mistakes, make corrections, and move on with life. Look forward. Your future is not in the past.

When you find yourself wanting to give up, wanting to quit, ask yourself this question: Why am I doing this? What is my goal? Then, do what you have to do to get where you want to go. Stop worrying about your personal paparazzi: your friends and distant relatives who see snapshots of your life but don't really understand you. Don't fear their two-dimensional, average opinion of your multidimensional, exceptional aspirations.

Remember your purpose. I cannot emphasize this enough. Move in the direction of your goals and only in that direction. Don't let others' negative opinions determine your value. No one can put a price on you. You're worth what you believe you're worth.

Do you know the definition of a slave? There was a time when African slaves were considered to be three-fifths of a person. (Some people still think of women in that way, or there would not be a statistically proven, gender-based wage disparity for doing the same work in many industries.) When most Americans think of slavery, they think of shackles and the eleven million Africans who survived the journey to the New World in the filthy, dark bellies of massive ships. They think of cotton plantations, the Underground Railroad, and the Civil War.

That is a poignant, but narrow, definition of slavery. According to Webster's dictionary, a slave is "a person who is under the domination of some influence or person." Today, that person or influence may have another name, but if your Boo (your sweetheart) always decides where you go, what you do, and when you leave, it's reasonable to infer you are a "slave." If you're draining your bank account to single digits every month by purchasing new clothing because some magazine says it's a "must have for the upcoming fashion season," then, by definition, you're a slave, too. If you skip school or blow off studying for an exam that could help you garner a promotion because your friend says it's ladies' night at the club… Hmmm? Any questions?

When we allow our decisions to be dictated or influenced by other people without considering our own best interests or the repercussions on our family, then we have a slave mentality, and that bling, bling is nothing but a rhinestone shackle chaining us to a future filled with debt and anxiety.

Everything matters. Each choice you make, person you encounter, or action you fail to take affects your destiny. And the wrong choices actually change your destiny. When it's time to select your future, never choose fear.

WEAR YOUR SUNDAY SHOES ON TUESDAY

Be bold. Be cutting edge. Be a candle in the darkness. Be anything but ordinary! Ordinary is boring. It's like caressing your own arm. It does not leave a lasting impression. Strive to leave an impression as unique as your fingerprints on everyone you encounter.

Coincidence is when someone else notices your preparation.

When I was young, I had Sunday clothes, including those special, white, patent leather, once-a-week shoes. Those relatively expensive and eternally shiny shoes were donned only on special occasions such as attending recitals and church. I was not allowed to wear my shoes for jumping rope or bike riding. The shoes were reserved for formal gatherings for reasons only cultural historians and my mother could explain. Invariably, I outgrew those special shoes after wearing them a few times. Poor return for the investment, one might conclude. When my toes could no longer bear the pressure, the shoes went to a younger cousin or Goodwill and eventually tortured another child with their shiny prohibitions.

There are two reasons I share stories like this one. First, I have no stories from the Hamptons or Martha's Vineyard that would make a bit of difference in your life. Secondly, I know a positive *and* lasting first impression usually leads to a second opportunity. Anyone can make a *good* first impression. Show up, dress nicely, speak well, and use the right fork. Good impression. But will they remember you tomorrow or even later this evening? How do you make that good impression last?

Start by emphasizing your strengths. They may be external or internal, but they belong to you. Use them. If you are smart, be smart. Do not be arrogant or condescending, but punctuate the conversation with thought-provoking opinions supported by facts. If you're funny, make them laugh. If you're an average conversationalist, be an above average fashionista. Go to vintage shops. Get discount codes online by putting in key words like "Macy's" and "coupon." Mix and match what you already own. It's not mandatory that you always wear your red blazer with the same red skirt. The designer will not stalk and rebuke you. Rock the red jacket with your five-year-old black skirt and the gold Michael Kors belt you borrowed from your mother's closet six months ago. If you can afford *haute couture* paid in cash (or you really cannot afford it) allow your personal shopper to put you in colors and styles you have avoided in the past. Maintain a professional image that makes you stand out from the herd.

A popular, female Texas politician tells the story of showing up at her first legislative session wearing a dark suit, similar to the style her male colleagues favored. Her female mentor, a seasoned politico, pulled the young politician aside and advised her never to wear black or navy again because she wouldn't be noticed in the crowd. She followed the advice, favoring bright colors. Subsequently, the media picked her up in almost every televised event and she became highly sought after for comments despite her rookie status in Washington. She went on to have a legendary career, and she credits this small change as making a major difference.

Remember, people see you before they hear you. Be bold with your hair, your clothes, and your attitude. Exude confidence from every angle. Create a well-rounded image that is easy to recall.

There is a caveat, however, and that is, if you want to fit in, do not stand out in a way that says, "No way, no how, does she belong to this group." To illustrate the importance of this rule, let's look at the story of Madison, who worked as an intern at a large law firm many years ago. The young woman, who was from a small Texas town, was charming, pleasant, and diligent during her internship, hoping it might lead to a permanent position within the organization. However, she had one small, yet brilliantly outstanding feature: a silver crown on her right front tooth with her initials carved on it.

A partner in the firm who was from the same small town sat her down for a private chat during her last week in the office.

The one-way conversation went like this: "Like you, love your work, but if you want a job offer, lose the silver crown." Madison was advised that the conservative organization she sought to be a part of would not cite her smile as a reason for not extending her a job offer, but that was one major strike against her. This advice was proffered tactfully and with the best intentions, but the young woman felt insulted by the self-appointed mentor. When she left, with a huff and a puff, it was as though she had never been there, because sadly, she stood out from the crowd a tad too much.

Years later, she popped up at an intern recruiting session. She was a successful practicing lawyer seeking law students to work in her office. When she smiled, wide and friendly, it was apparent that bygones were bygones. So was the silver crown.

So, I tell you to be authentic and then suggest you not be too authentic? Is that what you're thinking? The lessons are flexible, and you must be, as well, my friend. There are norms and standards we should not ignore, particularly when we are new to the environment. An African-American woman with natural hair, for example, is now accepted in the workplace. Twenty years ago, neither an afro nor a robin's egg blue blazer would have been welcome in the executive suites of most large companies. New companies emerged that emphasized the appearance of their product more than the appearance of their personnel, and the paradigm shifted. Successful women lead from the cutting edge, but they do not get so far ahead of the company culture that they become a distraction to the mission. Unless you are an entertainer, profits and productivity should be the main subject at the office, not your appearance.

LESSON THREE SUMMARY

☞ Self-esteem, self-respect, and self-love are prerequisites to self-actualization.

☞ Every choice you make moves you toward or away from your destiny.

☞ Emphasize your strengths.

☞ Take fear in healthy doses, not too much or too little.

☞ Always focus on the future. The future is not in your past.

☞ An indelible first impression opens the door to opportunity.

☞ Be authentic, but know which rules you should not break.

Lesson Four:
Sun Up 'til Sundown

ONE OF MY favorite sayings is "Claim It All You Want, But Where Is Your Receipt?" That means it takes more than prayer to achieve your goals. It takes work, which implies movement of some type. People, like objects, can move in a variety of directions. Don't mistake horizontal or lateral movement for forward progress. The major enemies of reaching our goals are reminiscing instead of doing, and analyzing instead of acting.

CLAIM IT ALL YOU WANT

After Sunday church service, Mrs. Jones took her daughter to the altar. She told the pastor her daughter was sick. The three of them knelt, and the pastor made a passionate plea to God, asking him to heal the child. As the mother and daughter stood and began to walk away, the pastor stopped them. He gently put his hand on the mother's shoulder and asked, "But you are going to take her to a doctor, right?"

You can ask for health, a bigger house, successful children, or what have you all you want, but action must accompany your faith before you will achieve your desires.

"Name it and claim it" is similar to the law of attraction. Having a strong optimism that you will accomplish what you set out to do is the critical first step toward success. Convincing yourself that you're capable of achieving your goals is invaluable in situations where the odds are against you or the failure of others who have tried to do the same thing is well documented.

Combining faith and action attracts people and opportunities that we didn't even know existed. Things happen that would not have occurred otherwise. When we repeatedly and consistently apply positive dynamism to change our lives, the magnetic force field we create will ultimately align with other positive forces.

Wanting without work, positive thinking without work, high self-esteem without work, amounts to nothing more than a song that doesn't rhyme and that only works for Celine Dion. This is not a new concept; it's plain old common sense, but unfortunately, common sense is not in vogue. (Take your pick. It's not popular and it's not in *Vogue* magazine.)

It's tempting to be seduced by the "name it and claim it" phenomenon, but anyone who's bought something on layaway knows it's not quite that simple. Before credit cards became so popular, layaway was the primary method that stores used to allow shoppers to buy things they couldn't afford. Purchases bought on the layaway plan are paid off in installments. The difference between layaway and credit cards is that layaway purchases must be paid in full before the shopper receives possession of them.

For that reason, spur-of-the-moment purchases were rare; people planned in advance to buy their children's back-to-school clothes or Christmas gifts. In midsummer, the layaway lines in stores began forming; people chose or "claimed" the things they wanted and paid a deposit to have the store hold the items for them. Someone who claimed something by putting it in layaway did not automatically get the item. Over the next few weeks or months, shoppers methodically paid down their balances on the items they wanted. As the first day of school or Christmas approached, those who were disciplined about making their payments on time stood in line for the last time, receipts in hand, prepared to physically claim their goods. Those who did not fulfill their payment commitments over time did not even bother to show up. They knew that the items they had claimed, but failed to pay for, went back into the inventory.

Don't expect rewards without sacrifice.

A few stores still have layaway, but many have forgotten the layaway mentality of paying for the things we want. Today, we set our expectations high in every category—great job, great home and car, great life—and we get indignant when the rewards we expect do not come our way immediately. The concept of striving for the rewards by putting in the time along with intellectual and physical effort seems old-fashioned, almost irrelevant. People expect dividends without making a significant investment. Think about the too-good-to-be-true offers of online degrees that require no homework or the mini-mansions with no down payments. We've seen the dire results of possession without payment.

So, how do you turn positive thinking into a possession? First, be realistic about what you claim. Get beyond the simpleminded idea that being realistic means you are not aiming high enough. You cannot fly a kite forty feet in the air if you only have twenty feet of string, no matter how high you aim. Being realistic starts with taking inventory of the tools at your disposal to help you get what you want. Determine how to get your hands on that extra twenty feet of string if you want to fly high. The tools you need to make your dreams come true might include money, time, education, skills, and support systems. If there is ever a time to be hard on yourself, to be merciless in your evaluation, it is when you go through your personal tool kit. You might as well acknowledge what you lack because, sooner or later, real life or the repo man will tap you on the back and educate you about your shortcomings.

Now abandon the hard-core attitude that was so useful in taking inventory and turn on the optimistic left side of your brain. To this day, sometimes the list of things I need to accomplish my goals is so time-consuming or complicated that I can get tired just thinking about it. It's easy to feel overwhelmed, then discouraged, and before you know it, to drop your quest for success. Don't give up! As they say, the only way to eat an elephant is one bite at a time!

In the beginning, single-focus, meaning slice that huge goal into manageable, small bites. It is better to meet one small goal than to tackle three and get nothing done. Carve out an easy-to-accomplish task like getting an assumed name certificate which is a business name that is different from your personal name. It is usually referred to by the legal term "doing business as" and abbreviated DBA. In most U.S. counties, an unincorporated business or profession that regularly conducts business or provides professional services must file a DBA with the County Clerk so that a record of the business is established. The registration form is easy to fill out and the filing fees are budget friendly. Then select another challenge, such as ordering business cards, and complete it. Once you gain momentum and confidence, reaching your ultimate goal will be so much easier.

Don't doubt that you can have the things you want out of life, because you can. Simply be willing to do the hard work and exercise the patience to earn your reward by consistently paying the price a little at a time.

PREMATURE AGING SYNDROME
(TOO MUCH EMPHASIS ON THE PAST)

Many women spend way too much time remembering the things they should forget, wasting time embracing the moments they regret. Don't become preoccupied with your failures. Learn the lessons of your mistakes, make corrections, and move on with life. Always look forward.

Your future is not in the past.

Florence Chadwick is permanently tattooed in history as the first woman to swim in both directions across the English Channel. Do you know how frickin' far that is? It's pretty far because, in 1950, it took her thirteen hours to swim from France to England; later, because she could, she swam sixteen hours from England to France! I could write another book on why few people recall Chadwick's amazing accomplishments. However, the lesson we can learn from Chadwick is what happened *after* this American swimmer became famous around the world. In 1952, she attempted to swim from Santa Catalina Island to the California coast, about twenty-two miles. She gave up one mile short of the shore after hours in shark-infested water on a cold, foggy day. One mile. Had she gone home to dry and cry, believing no one had accomplished the feat because it could not be done—by a woman—she could have lived the rest of her life resting on the laurels of her English Channel world record.

Many of us give up when faced with seemingly insurmountable challenges and console ourselves with achievements. Others wallow in their past mistakes, wrongly believing their best years are behind them.

Chadwick did neither. She tried again. This time the weather conditions were once again abysmal, and the journey was difficult, but Chadwick swam that last mile to shore. The difference, she reportedly said, is that she saw the shoreline "in her mind."

Behold the results of persistence, and understand that the past and the future are simply mind games. The one you play is the one you choose. Am I saying you must completely forget your past in order to accomplish your future purpose? No. Forgetting all your past condemns you to repeating it. I'm suggesting that you put more emphasis on "yes, I can" instead of "no, I could never." Imagine what effect that would have on your life.

ANALYSIS PARALYSIS *(WORRYING ABOUT THE FUTURE/CONSEQUENCES)*

Danish philosopher Kierkegaard said anxiety about the unknown is *dread,* as opposed to worrying about a known entity, which is *fear.* Call it what you want. The most common reason we hesitate to act is because we don't want to fail. Again, success is not achieved without taking risks. Walking across the street involves several risks: getting hit by a motor vehicle, tripping in the street, spraining your ankle stepping off the curb, bumping into another pedestrian. You're smiling because it is unlikely any of these things will happen, but it is possible. You are willing to take this real, but remote, risk because you need to reach a destination. Well, you also need to move forward with your life, and that involves taking risks. You can't anticipate everything. That's why we have hindsight. Make plans, make contingency plans, say a prayer, and make a move.

Success is not achieved without taking risk.

Let's use teenagers in general as an example, and in particular, boys, who are fearless. Having raised two very typical boys who are now in their midtwenties, I feel comfortable saying I know a little bit about the developing male psyche. Boys will try anything, from water surfing during a hurricane to riding a skateboard down a stair rail, with little thought about negative consequences. Actuaries, the people who do seem to know "the day and the hour" of Jesus's return, analyze statistics and recommend high premiums for male drivers ages sixteen to twenty-five because they are involved in a disproportionate number of motor vehicle accidents. Yet, we continue to let sixteen- to twenty-five-year-old males drive because the benefits of this demographic group having transportation are greater than the risks.

Caution is always in order. For example, while driving, there is something good and noble about staying in your lane until signaling your intention to change lanes. Still, it is annoying to be in the car with drivers who turn on the blinker ten miles before they finally accumulate the courage to move over. They're worrying about oncoming cars. They're concerned about the glare from the hood. The seat belt is too tight, and they have difficulty looking over their shoulder. Or they simply want to talk about changing lanes until you scream, voluntarily open the passenger door, and fling yourself in front of oncoming traffic.

Successful women consider the flow of traffic, the acceleration ability of their vehicle, the condition of the road, and the weather before they make a decision. But then—they make a decision and make something happen. Even the best business plan cannot anticipate everything good or bad that might happen. No business with SBA financing would ever fail if that were true. Frankly, there is a degree of luck involved in every successful venture that is undeniable.

When I invested in a Mediterranean restaurant in downtown Fort Worth a few years ago, I did so knowing the venture could fail, but believing it would succeed. Why was I optimistic? The general manager was experienced, and he had worked at several four-star eating establishments. The general partner came from a family of restaurateurs, and the other partners in the corporation we formed were all successful business professionals like me. And, the restaurant was located on the ground floor of a beautiful glass building, a former bank, in the heart of downtown with six-figure condos occupied by busy people. My accountant and attorney gave me a thumbs-up on the business plans, but they did warn me that new restaurants are risky.

Armed with these facts, I cautiously invested money I did not want to lose, but it was money I could lose and still survive (assuming I kept my day job.) A few months later, the recession kicked in, and despite heroic efforts, we closed after less than three years in business. Talk about humbling. All of my closest friends and several family members had come to our grand opening. Granted, my sons had told me they hated the food, but they were teenagers so I ignored their ominous review. Lesson learned. Do I regret losing my money? Yes. Do I regret a calculated, well-researched try? No. I will continue to take evidence-based risks rather than be paralyzed into waiting my entire life on a statistically impossible can't-fail venture.

......

Most (people) prefer lives of quiet desperation to the possible embarrassment of trying and failing to realize their heart's desire. ~Harriet Lerner, PhD

......

"Analysis paralysis" is an informal phrase used so commonly it is actually an article in *Wikipedia*. If you suffer from analysis paralysis, you're wondering how to determine when you've done enough research, asked enough questions, and made enough preparation to venture toward your individual destiny. Try using this admissions test:

1. When you've talked in depth to everyone you know and at least five experts in the industry in question,

2. *and* you have a written, detailed plan of action (or business plan) that includes a time line,

3. *and* you've attended at least two educational classes (not sales presentations) on the subject or interned at a similar place of business,

4. *and* you've read (not skimmed through) three or more books by different authors about it,

5. *and* you can answer every question from every critic, especially your family members, excluding your parents (who will ask questions forever because they love you and don't want you to move back in with them),

6. *and* you've found a knowledgeable, successful mentor who is willing to walk you through the unexpected and unknowns,

7. *and* after six to twelve months of preparation, you still can't sleep because of your excitement about the future...

Then, go for it! Sure, you might fail, but you might successfully cross the street, and who knows what great things await you on the other side?

Need a little on-demand inspiration? Try reading these powerful books (about turning setbacks into comebacks):

❖ *Falling Forward: How to Make the Most of Your Mistakes,* by John C. Maxwell (2000)

❖ *Unstoppable: 45 Powerful Stories of Perseverance and Triumph from People Just Like You,* by Cynthia Kersey (1998)

❖ *Extraordinary Comebacks: 201 Inspiring Stories of Courage, Triumph, and Success,* by John Sarkett (2007)

❖ *The Secret to Success Is Not a Secret: Stories of Famous People Who Persevered,* by Darcy Andries (2008)

LESSON FOUR SUMMARY

☞ Use a disciplined, systematic approach to achieving large goals. Dissect your objective into smaller, manageable tasks.

☞ Don't be preoccupied with your past failures.

☞ Success is not achieved without taking risks. Don't expect rewards without sacrifice unless it's Christmas or your birthday.

☞ Worry is not work. Rewarding work is the antidote to worry.

☞ Avoid "analysis paralysis" or overpreparation.

Lesson Five:
Change Your Mind

IGNORANCE IS NOT bliss. It's an invitation to be taken advantage of on a continual basis. Reading is the fertile territory where the hunt for wisdom begins. New information is brain food. Read at school, at work, on the Metro, in the bathroom—wherever. A woman who doesn't read is starving her intellect.

MOST IMPORTANT HABIT FOR SUCCESS

Reading is the most important habit of successful people. Reading is so critical to success that, historically, education has been limited to the ruling class, aka "the males" of almost every society, including the United States, Europe, India, Asia, and Africa. In some areas of the world, this academic discrimination is not a distant memory.

A January 2008 article in *Time* magazine discussed the "girl gap" in Afghanistan, resulting from the Taliban's policy of prohibiting girls from learning to read. Under that regime, toppled by allied forces in 2001, Afghan girls risked death to get an education. Sadly, in 2012, despite Western intervention, a fifteen-year-old girl named Malala Yousafzai was shot in the head at point-blank range by members of the Taliban for advocating that girls get an education. The author of the *Time* article concluded, "The stakes for Afghan society are high. Every social and economic index shows that countries with a higher percentage of women with a high school education also have better overall health, a more functional democracy, and increased economic performance."

....

Reading is fertilizer for the mind.

....

We have no excuse comparable to a death threat for not relentlessly pursuing knowledge. Exercising one's inalienable right to read is not a luxury sacrificed in the interest of time. It is a privilege to be indulged at every opportunity. That is why we must become compulsive and voracious readers. Reading gives us access to new information from a variety of sources not systematically diluted and politicized into editorial commentary rather than objective facts.

Most people read to *find* thoughts. They are content with adopting those thoughts as *their* thoughts. Empowerment comes when we read to *form* thoughts. In other words, don't count on someone else to provide an opinion for you. Gather knowledge from philosophers, scientists, economists, religious scholars, social activists, and anyone who puts pen to paper. Like a recipe made from scratch, use the best ingredients to create unique, personalized convictions of your own creation.

....

Read to form *opinions, not find them.*

....

Furthermore, if you learn new information or have a personal experience that changes what you've come to believe, do something most women never, ever learn to do. This is very important, so I'm mentioning it many times throughout this book. Read the next sentence slowly, multiple times. **You have an inalienable right to change your mind or modify your position.** That is part of maturing. Most children think reindeer can fly because their loving parents convince them this is so. If one never encounters a flying reindeer as an adult, it's reasonable to conclude they are now extinct. Remember, thoughts, like recipes, can always be improved upon by adding or deleting ingredients. Start your intellectual growth spree by taking your mental shopping cart to the idea store where everything is free and you won't do any damage to your credit score.

EXTRA CREDIT
....

Here's a small example of how you can benefit financially from reading something as mundane as a mail insert. I was considering switching cable companies and bundling my cable with my Internet and home phone service. By my rough calculation, the cost of the bundle would be cheaper than the individual services, leading to significant savings over a few years. However, my main reason for switching was the potential convenience of having one provider and one bill. One afternoon after work, I stopped by the storefront of the company I was considering as my new provider to get some information. The salesman was very helpful. He even gave me a demonstration of the numerous features of his company's cable service. He went so far as to offer me a monthly credit of nineteen dollars for one year and a one-hundred-dollar rebate to cover the cost of switching! He dangled that bait so skillfully I almost bit, but...hmmm, something told me to investigate this great bargain.

Back home, I recalled getting a postcard in the mail a few weeks earlier encouraging me to switch to the new company. I'd skimmed it before I tossed it in the trash. I remembered reading something about a gift card, but the salesman at the store hadn't mentioned anything about it. I surfed to the company's website. Guess what? If I signed up for one of their bundles online, I would still get nineteen dollars a month credit for one year, plus *two hundred* dollars cash back, and a twenty-five-dollar Visa gift card. It took ten minutes max to sign up online with the new company.

Can I buy a Maserati with a little windfall like this? No, not a real one, but I could add a little more to my IRA or enjoy a nice dinner with my family. Opportunities like this happen all the time, especially in this economy. Companies are desperate for your business, and they're making all sorts of great offers like cash back, rebates, and free stuff that most people never notice because they don't read the fine print or take a few minutes to compare offers. Over time, taking a few moments to do a little research comparing companies or looking for discounts can save you a lot of money.

I know you cannot and should not spend hours shopping around every time you buy a candy bar. Definitely, shop around when you're making a large purchase or a long-term commitment where a contract is involved. You should know it's going to cost $3,000 to terminate your vehicle lease early or if there is a prepay penalty on your mortgage. Don't let anyone rush you into signing or buying anything without reading through the agreement and asking as many questions as you need to in order to understand the commitment you are making. If they pressure you, walk away. The deal of a lifetime comes along every day. You will never become financially secure by throwing away hundreds or thousands of dollars because you won't take the time to do the same due diligence for yourself that you would in renewing or negotiating a contract for your employer or your parents.

Ladies, be leery when someone brags to you, "I don't read" or "I don't have time to read" or "I only read X." That's like saying, "I don't ever want to learn anything on my own again." If the government of the United States takes control of all publications and refuses to print any article without Uncle Sam's preapproval, what would we do? Yell "censorship"? March on Washington? Start a petition no one will read? We would all have some type of negative reaction because Americans value the freedom of receiving information, which is intimately connected to our constitutional right to free speech. Okay, you don't want all your news from the government, but that's very similar to having it spoon-fed from your favorite news anchor or talk show host because you don't take time to read other sources. What's the difference? You still get all your information from one outlet. Media companies must be sensitive to the reactions of advertisers and subscribers because advertisements and subscriptions pay the bills.

You are not going to find a totally unbiased, unbought source of information, but getting your news from multiple places gives you multiple perspectives to consider. In this Internet age, it is possible to read newspaper articles, blogs, journals, and books from around the world. Believe me, you'll impress the heck out of your boss or blind date when you mention the article you read in *The Daily Mirror*, a British newspaper. That's what I call "positive gossip": the kind of small talk that makes you stand out from the crowd.

As entertaining as it is to watch *YouTube* and satellite television, it is impossible for a ten-minute video or a half-hour broadcast to truly convey the horror of South Africa's apartheid as depicted in Mark Mathabane's autobiography *Kaffir Boy*. In fact, fiction transports you into the lives of people residing in places you may never have an opportunity to visit. Two bestselling books of historical fiction, *Memoirs of a Geisha* (Kyoto, Japan) and *The Kite Runner* (Afghanistan), introduced millions of readers to the traditions of countries often ignored in Western press unless we're at war.

....

Do one thing every day that scares you.
~ Eleanor Roosevelt

....

It is difficult to find any influential leader, present or past, who lacks a thirst for knowledge. The list of women who have risen to positions of prominence on the magic carpet of books is endless. Retired Associate Justice Sandra Day O'Conner, the first woman to serve on the US Supreme Court; Pam Iorio, fifty-seventh mayor of Tampa, Florida; and Dr. Beverly Daniel Tatum, president of Spelman College, are a few examples of accomplished women who make time to read, despite their demanding schedules.

Reading is *not* optional. Read a minimum of one book a month that is not directly related to your job or favorite pastime, and I guarantee it will be the most lucrative investment you'll ever make in your future. If time is a factor, try audiobooks while you drive or work out.

Fertilize your mind with knowl-
edge and your life will flourish!

---

120 HOURS TO THE LIFE YOU DESERVE

In a banquet hall filled with people, the featured speaker might be the most accomplished person present, but the odds are high she is not the person with the most raw intelligence or natural gifts. The person with the quickest mind or the most talent could easily be the events planner who organized the affair or the waiter serving the dinner rolls. Statistics are not necessary to verify this point; think about the people you interact with daily and the members of your family who are actually quite brilliant. You know the ones, the problem-solving administrative assistant who makes you look smarter than you ever will be, or your quiet cousin who has spent her life changing diapers following her perfect SAT score in high school.

Maybe you are the unheralded genius in the bunch. If your manager consistently seeks your opinion before making decisions, if you regularly spot and (humbly) correct the mistakes of others, or if you're always the first one to clearly see the solution to problematic situations, then you might be the smartest person in the room. If so, do your job and salary parallel your natural abilities, or do your coworkers and friends have better positions and make more money than you do? If you perceive that discrepancy as a problem, what is the reason you haven't reached your personal best?

If your rewards are not equal to your talent, you must determine why or you will never excel.

The reason is likely that you haven't dedicated 120 hours to dramatically increasing your earning potential. Spending fifteen hours a week, taking classes for four years, equals approximately 120 hours and a framed college degree on the wall. Today, it is not unusual to hear people, even people who have college educations, say that a college degree is not necessary to be successful. That statement makes about as much sense as saying a person can get around Los Angeles without a car. Yes, it can be done, but why make life so hard?

Enrolling in college is easy; graduating is the challenge.

My parents were sticklers for education. They were unyielding in their efforts to ensure their children, grandchildren, and great grands graduated from high school, then went on to learn a specific skill set leading to financial independence. Being tired from the part-time jobs we worked or lacking interest in school was not an acceptable excuse for failing to do our very best in every subject.

Those looking for an excuse to avoid additional education will point to Microsoft founder Bill Gates, or rapper and mogul Jay Z, or someone else who succeeded without earning a degree. Before you buy into that argument, do some investigating. Visit www.microsoft.com/careers and see whom the company is hiring these days. The first thing you'll notice is that if you want to work for Microsoft, you are competing with people in China, Denmark, India, Egypt, Germany, and other places around the world. Your competitor in India is not relying on what she learned in high school to land a job with Microsoft. Next, research some of the available jobs. You will see, again and again, "Computer science degree preferred." Do not let the word *preferred* mislead you. If a company interviews two equally bright people and one has a master's degree in computer science while the other one has only a high-school diploma, guess who gets the job.

Educational programs exist for every budget, so while you are on Microsoft's site, go ahead and search for scholarships. You will see that the company offers one-year free-ride scholarships, but to qualify you must be enrolled in a college or university.

During the recent recession, there were a lot of true stories about college graduates with MBAs and PhDs who were unemployed. True, no one is immune to layoffs or firing. However, when the economy recovers and companies begin hiring, typically those with advanced knowledge earn higher wages. Additionally, the exposure and mental stimulation of learning are so appealing that many stars have gone to college *after* becoming famous, including *Harry Potter* star Emma Watson, Dakota Fanning, Shaq O'Neal, America Ferrera of *Ugly Betty*, Sandra Bullock, and Oscar Warner.

The online edition of the *Houston Chronicle published* the average salary of several groups of potential wage earners in the section on career advice (http://work.chron.com/average-salary-college-degree-1861.html).

Here are the results, which used data from the US Bureau of Labor Statistics 2011 report:

➤ high school dropouts: $451 per week (median annual salary $21,000 since 1995)

➤ high school diploma: $638 per week

➤ associate's degree: $768 per week

➤ bachelor's degree: $1,053 per week

➤ master's degree: $1,263 per week

....
Additional education after high school is
an investment in your future.
....

Using those numbers, let's take an imaginary look at three friends; Vanna Masters, Derrick Bachelors, and Ava Ged. Assume they are equally intelligent and hard working. After high school, Vanna Masters and Derrick Bachelors go to college, and Ava Ged starts work. Vanna M. and Derrick B. earn college degrees; then

Vanna M. continues to get an advanced degree, while Derrick B. joins the work force.

Over their lifetimes, Derrick B.'s four-year degree will bring him $800,000 more than Ava G. makes as a high school graduate. Vanna M.'s advanced degree translates to $200,000 more than Derrick B. makes and $1,000,000 (let's repeat that)—*one frickin' million dollars more* than Ava G. earns! Yep, one million dollars additional earned income, even though Ava G. has a six-year head start as an employee.

The benefits of education are not only in cash. Vanna M., now in management, has excellent benefits such as health insurance, a retirement plan, and disability benefits, whereas Ava G. is sometimes covered by insurance and other times not. Ava G. cannot always afford well-woman exams, and unfortunately, the lack of top-notch medical care might result in a late diagnosis of high cholesterol or hypertension.

Derrick B.'s employer has one of the best retirement plans in the nation, and he contributes the maximum allowed. His nest egg multiplies over the years, despite an occasional economic downturn. Ava G. has a 401(k) also, and she contributes what she can after meeting her expenses, but her balance lags far below Derrick B.'s, partly because she cannot afford a financial planner to help her invest.

The effects of choices made by Vanna M., Derrick B., and Ava G., don't end there. According to Carol Colett of CEOs for Cities, having college graduates as residents "is the best predictor for economic success" of a city. Therefore, having a college education affects the neighborhoods you live in, the quality of education your children receive, and the quality of your health as you age.

Speaking of age, delete the excuse that you are too old to go back to school. Mature students are often the best students because they have put their time and their own money on the line and don't intend to fail. As the saying goes, next year you will be one year older regardless of how you spend those 365 days.

While this section emphasizes the benefits of a college degree, the overarching goal of continuing education is obtaining a degree of completion, a license, or certification, not solely "going to college." Businessman Robert Kiyosaki, bestselling author of the *Rich Dad, Poor Dad* series of self-help books, says formal education leads many to an employee mentality of wanting a salary and paid vacations. He places high value on life skills and the important lessons learned from experience in the real world. The key to real wealth is business ownership and investing in real estate, according to him. I do not disagree that ownership and good investments lead to wealth accumulation, with or without advanced education. However, Kiyosaki attended the US Merchant Marine Academy after high school and graduated as a deck officer in 1969. Academy graduates earn a bachelor of science degree.

WHILE YOU'RE LEARNING...

I've talked about the importance of reading habitually, but there are a few other skills I suggest adding to your personal growth portfolio. While these skills may not seem to apply directly to your life or job, everyone I interviewed for this book agreed they are lifesavers for surviving the deep waters of leadership.

❖ Time Management (It's an art form, and more than simply juggling multiple tasks.)

❖ Anger Management (I personally love the book *Anger Management for Dummies*. Note: suppressing anger and passive-aggressive behavior are as self-destructive as yelling.)

❖ Basic Etiquette (Prospective employers and those with whom you interact socially do judge your social grace whether they tell you or not.)

❖ Sales (Service, product, or ideas—it's all sales.)

❖ Conflict Resolution (We negotiate and mediate with everyone. Learn to do it skillfully, whether buying a car or a franchise.)

❖ ABCs of Human Resources (Legalities apply to babysitters and part-time employees, among others.)

❖ Public Speaking (Unless all your words are in your head, learning to speak in public is essential. Overcome the fear.)

❖ Finance (Basic accounting is essential for your home budget and your company's bottom line. You cannot meet your revenue/savings goals if you don't track financial data and use metrics to make fiscally sound decisions.)

HIT THE ROAD, JACK

The top two reasons people give for not exploring America the beautiful or venturing overseas are lack of time and money. By the time you finish reading this book, you will know how to manage your time and save money. So assume time and money are not a problem. The third reason women hesitate to travel may be due to their addiction to the familiar. Knowing what to expect is comforting to the average person, so much so that we will accept the same boring routine every day, whether it's an uninteresting job or an unfulfilling relationship.

Traveling, especially outside the country, is a big step away from the familiar. Going abroad means losing control over situations that you may have (or think you have) control over in your day-to-day routine. Be willing to examine the flip side of fear. Exploring the planet and getting to know more about the people on it will give you the courage to face the unknown wherever you encounter it. As you see the beauty in other places, you may also begin to see more beauty in other people.

Visiting an area adds richness to your spirit that Google Earth simply cannot convey. Seeing ancient ruins or modern wonders of the world confirms the ingenuity of the human race. Talking to people about their lifestyles and their worldviews will help you better understand issues ranging from economics to foreign affairs.

We have all heard the term *Ugly American,* which was used to describe US citizens traveling abroad. A more fitting title might be *Ignorant American* because rude behavior is often rooted in the ignorance that accompanies lack of exposure. Travel transforms us into *Educated Americans* because when we travel, we automatically learn new things, even if we simply venture to another US state. Southerners who are accustomed to traveling coast-to-coast do not starve because there is no fried catfish on the LA Café's menu—if they approach cuisine with an open mind, grilled halibut or blackened scallops taste mighty fine, y'all.

It is critical to learn all you can about where you are visiting before you go. Many websites, such as www.lonelyplanet.com, provide basic overviews of cities and countries. The overviews give you insight on what to expect and what to avoid. Guidebooks by experts like Rick Steves also suggest must-see places and must-have experiences. Most travel guides now have apps for your phone or tablet, making them as easy to carry abroad as a pocket-sized, personal travel guide. Learn about the history, currency, and climate of the place you are visiting in advance for a much better adventure during your trip.

LIFELINE

When I visited Paris with my parents and sister recently, I expected to meet the stereotypical "rude" French people I'd heard so much about. In fact, I had studiously avoided traveling to France for years because the people of France have such a huge reputation in America for being unpleasant. Luckily, I went online for travel tips and learned that many of the French consider Americans rude, also. For example, the way we begin conversations and queries without a greeting. In America, it's not uncommon to ask a salesperson, "Uhm, where are the women's blouses?" or a passerby, "Is there an ATM around here?" In France, they prefer, *"Bonjour,* please tell me how to get to the Louvre?"

Seriously, I went to Paris knowing two words of French: *bonjour* and *merci*—good morning and thank you. (I don't think Chardonnay counts, does it?) The surprisingly friendly French, including those who didn't speak English, went out of their way to help my family. They just laughed when I said *bonjour* (good morning) at night. They laughed and helped me anyway. We did not have one incidence of rudeness from anyone. I learned two things. Learning about a country's culture and customs can really make the difference during travel. And, there are no unattractive people in France. It's the weirdest thing.

**

Whether you are going across the country to Seattle or halfway around the world to Singapore, you should learn this French phrase: *vive la difference.* Roughly translated, the phrase means long live the difference, or celebrate the difference. The places you visit are not going to be just like home and the people you meet are not going to be cultural duplicates of the people you already know. The very reason travel is a great way to learn is because it exposes us to new and different experiences. As long as you are prepared to celebrate, rather than fight the differences, you can have a good time. *Oui, oui!*

And please don't let your age be a deterrent. My Grandma Lucile traveled to Cuba and Japan to visit her children at US military bases when she was in her sixties, and my parents have been overseas multiple times after entering their seventh and eighth decades of life. As long as your health permits, there is no age too old or too young to begin exploring the world.

....
Expand your tastes and relax your expectations.
....

When you travel, one of the main things to remain open-minded about is food. Food is important to Americans under ordinary circumstances and takes on greater importance when we're away from home. Television ads lure us into believing every meal should be delicious, romantic, and set against a breathtaking background. The stars of the cable channel cooking shows never have a meal they do not like, no matter how strange it looks! Throw in the temporary escape from grocery shopping, cooking, and clean-up duty, and our expectations of how much pleasure we will get from the food we eat on vacation are really, really high.

Blindfold your taste buds and relax your expectations. Don't avoid the local cuisine in order to eat American fast food while in the Caribbean, or at an ethnic restaurant in New York. Food cannot bite back (*jumiles,* otherwise known as live beetles, might be an exception), but you would never know that based on the way some of us stress out at the notion of trying something new. Don't be too intimidated to step out of your food box. Start by trying a dish that combines ingredients familiar to you in an unfamiliar way. For example, *feijoada, a* traditional Brazilian dish, is made with black beans and pork; if you have ever eaten pork and beans, then there would be no rational reason for you to be afraid to try *feijoada. Right?*

Next, talk the talk. Don't judge the dialect or language spoken by people you meet while traveling. Remember, Standard English is new, compared to most of the languages in the world. If you want to be labeled an Ugly American, complain about the lack of

English-speaking people in a country where English is not the most commonly used language. It is fine to ask whether there is a person at the hotel front desk who is fluent in English, but it is rude to complain if there is not. You can navigate any country in the world if you learn how to say three things in the native language: hello, please, and thank you. And when you are abroad, remember that communication is not solely about the spoken word. A smile and a friendly gesture can speak volumes in any country.

Finally, maybe you are willing to travel but you do not have a traveling companion. Fortunately, there are thousands of people just like you, who are interested in going to the same places. Finding an organized tour is easier than finding a pair of size 8.5 navy sling-backs at Macy's during a half-price sale.

No more excuses. No more delays. Treasures await the willing traveler.

LESSON FIVE SUMMARY

> Reading is the number one factor for success. It is fertilizer for the mind.

> Read to form original thoughts, not to find others' thoughts and claim them as their own.

> You have the right to change your mind. It is not a sign of weakness.

> Education increases your earning potential. It's an investment in your future.

> Use the flip side of fear to become more adventurous.

> Celebrate and embrace cultural differences.

> Being judgmental limits your opportunities for personal growth. The "right" way is usually just the popular way, but never the only way.

Lesson Six: Chase Paper

KEEPING MONEY IS much harder than making it. People win millions in the lottery and end up bankrupt a few years later because they do not have the *financial literacy* to manage their assets. Others have the financial literacy, but they will not commit to delaying immediate gratification for long-term security. Wealth building, aka paper-chasing strategies, range from home ownership, to home-based businesses, to building relationships with people who don't mistake liabilities for assets. Ultimately, billionaires like the Marses, Benettons, and Walton families best illustrate the key to building wealth. For generation after generation, they keep working for their money and making their money work for them.

WORK AT HOME

How to build wealth is the worst-kept secret in the history of capitalism. The secret is (drum roll, please) spend less than you earn. That's easier to read about than to do, and in fact, it's getting harder to do as cost of living increases consistently outpace salary increases for most employees. Consequently, many of us are spending our future retirement funds on our current car note. So what legal options do you have when a gap forms between your income and your expenses?

A. Get another part- or full-time job?

B. Invest in the stock market?

C. Give away your disobedient kid who really doesn't resemble you and keep the smart, quiet one?

Maybe, maybe, and, hmmmmm, okay, no.

There is no shame in working two jobs, and there are investments that carry less risk while historically earning more interest than a savings account at the local bank. Your financial adviser (get one if you don't already have one) should be able to give you guidance in this area. But, there is another way to make money where you set your own hours and have a more flexible schedule. It's a home-based business, and many successful corporations began in this manner. Martha Stewart, who, incidentally, graduated from Barnard with a double major, began her catering business at home after giving up a career as a stockbroker. The key to building your business is hard work, research/education, and networking.

It's not enough to be skilled in cookie baking. You must understand the industry and structure your business properly to minimize risk to your family. Sample scenario: A friend is helping fulfill a big cookie order. She slips in the kitchen or burns herself on the oven. Will your insurance cover her medical expenses? If a jealous neighbor calls the city and complains about the odor of milk chocolate permeating the neighborhood day and night, do you have the proper permits/licenses for a home-based business? Are you required to collect sales taxes?

....
You can't have cash equity without sweat equity.
....

In addition to exercising due diligence, involve legal and financial experts at every step of your venture. These planned investments prevent costly unplanned mistakes and fines. However, the wonderful benefit is that you can do what you like, when you like, and how you like—but, yes, it's still hard work.

Too many folks want the cash but not the sweat. They want an effortless life.

Accumulating wealth requires a financial roadmap to the future of your dreams. The best way to travel any road is to drive. Shift your life's gears and make a move. If you're headed into more debt, shift into reverse. If you're not moving, get out of neutral. If you seem to be spinning your wheels in a rut, try overdrive until the road is clear.

NO SPONSOR NEEDED

Do you have an expensive love? I'm not referring to a six-two athletic dream lover. Perhaps a low-slung, two-door convertible is your baby tonight. And why not? Most of you have sacrificed—missed a few parties, eaten a lot of cheap fast food, crammed all night—in order to be where you are today. After all that voluntary suffering, isn't a reward in order? Don't you deserve a shiny new luxury import to accent your designer sunglasses? That depends. Before you make that down payment, let's do a little math.

If you want to be an official graduate of leadership prep school, figuring out the real costs of things, which includes not only the dollars, but also, how much you forego in savings, has to become obsessive-compulsive behavior.

A coveted late-model Luxury Car XYZ, in Black Sapphire, costs $50,000 plus, without tax, title, and license. Suppose Miss "Almost in the Money" is down to her last two car notes of $300 each on a well-maintained, four-year-old vehicle. Miss Almost is driving along, minding her own business when the Black Sapphire XYZ pulls up next to her at a red light. Two months later, Miss Almost trades in her car for $2,000, kicks in a $3,000 down payment, and drives that beautiful, brand-new XYZ convertible off the lot. The payments on this new toy are over $1,060 a month for five years. Miss Almost, who was on the verge of being able to invest an extra $300 a month into her pathetically low, never-gonna-be-able-to-retire(ment) account, has just tripled the auto expense line in her budget. Well, what if Miss A recently got a raise, you might wonder. Financial guru Suze Orman suggests there are better ways to invest it, such as paying off student loans or high interest credit cards to increase your Fair Isaac Corporation (FICO) score that lenders use to determine your credit risk. With a good FICO, you will get a better interest rate on future purchases.

But I'm sure Suze has a nice car, possibly a driver, so back to our friend, Miss A. If every four years, she upgrades to a new ride, the amount of money she cannot save or invest in other things is absolutely mind blowing. Visit www.edmunds.com, an excellent website that calculates the true cost to own a car. The bottom line cost of the typical XYZ convertible is over $66,000. And get this: within a year of the front wheels hitting the pavement, the car depreciates over $9,000!

Financial counselors warn us that never-ending car notes are a major reason many of us cannot get out from behind the debt eight-ball. In addition to creating debt, getting a new car every three to five years hinders our goals of accumulating wealth. In her book, *Deal with Your Debt*, Liz Pulliam Weston states that keeping a car for ten years instead of five can put as much as $250,000 extra in your retirement account over your lifetime. Ten years may seem to be a long time to drive a compact car with factory rims, but there are other ways to roll with panache and save money at the same time if this is really important to you. Try buying certified used cars: luxury without the new car smell. Drive them six or seven years. At the very least, get a vehicle that gets good gas mileage and has low maintenance costs. Ask your insurance carrier how much the premiums will be before you buy the car, also. The answer varies from city to city, and it is something you want to know before you drive off the lot.

Here's one last example related to purchasing an auto. If you just gotta have it, you gotta have it. Fine. Here's where making better choices will save you money on that car note. The better your credit, the better interest rate the auto finance company *should* offer you on a new car. The note on a $30,000 vehicle at 3 percent interest is around $540 a month after a 10 percent down payment. For someone who must accept a 12 percent interest rate because of bad spending habits and high debt, tack on at least another hundred dollars a month for a whopping $670 a month difference. This is for the same car with the same down payment, ladies! That's an additional $1500 a year out of pocket because of that high interest rate. That's why it's important to shop around for all loans: mortgage, auto, credit cards...Companies do not always offer you the rate you qualify for even when you have stellar credit. Compare administrative fees and interest rates before you sign on the dotted line. Don't assume the dealer is offering you the best rate because you're a repeat customer or the salesman was friendly. And don't succumb to pressure tactics. Walk away if salespeople are patronizing, defensive, or unable to answer your questions.

Always calculate the real cost of your purchase, including maintenance.

Impulse spending, like emotional eating, is due to a lack of self-control. And like emotional eating, it is a very hard habit to break. Sometimes even smart women succumb to peer pressure (or passion) and spend money unwisely. If peer pressure is your weakness, remind yourself that things are not always as they appear. Calculate the true cost to own everything, not just your car.

One of the questions I ask my trend-setting mentees is "Do you have more invested in your wardrobe than your savings account?" Think about it. We all know women who purchase expensive clothes they can't afford to impress people they don't like, but they don't contribute to their employer-sponsored 401(k) plan or an individual retirement account (IRA). After the short-lived joy of gloating comes the long-term debt they must repay with interest. Don't sabotage yourself. People who do not like you on a visceral level will never like you. That's their problem. Meanwhile, we must conduct the business of our lives on facts, not emotions.

The purpose of not spending more than you earn is to ensure that you are financially secure at every stage of life. Spending wisely doesn't mean you never splurge—quite the opposite—the more you have in the bank, the easier it is to indulge in an occasional extravagance. Shop wisely; hunt for bargains on the web. I like Groupon and Internet sites like PriceGrabber.com. For large purchases or slightly damaged ones like a washing machine with a small scratch on the side, ask for discounts. Call your credit card companies and wireless carrier every six months to make sure you are getting the best rates. Put it on your calendar as a recurring date. It's worth the effort for the money you can save. I'm amazed at how many women don't take a few minutes to look for deals that will literally save them thousands of dollars over the course of a year because it's too much trouble. Working three jobs to pay off credit card debt is too much trouble. Filling out the FAFSA every year for student loans is trouble. Trust me. I know. Lesson learned.

Stone Age cave paintings illustrate men as hunters and women as child bearers who gathered fruit and vegetables. I wasn't there, but I'm guessing there were a lot more vegetarians, as wooly mammoths didn't come along every day. In other words, always be capable of feeding yourself. Think of yourself as a for-profit entity who doesn't need a sponsor but will gladly accept donations!

OWN SOMETHING

Owning something is a good idea—your home, the rental property, the mutual funds—because ownership brings security. Financial planners walk their clients through a series of steps to determine what is most important to the client. At the end of the forecast, most clients cite the desire to be independent for the rest of their lives. They want to be safe in old age, sheltered from crime, able to get the best health care, and living a slightly scaled-down version of their current lifestyle.

You have heard the phrase, "luck is opportunity meeting preparation." Owning something is a form of preparation. If you surround yourself with mentors and role models you can learn from, sooner or later you are going to be presented with an opportunity. For example, what if you're invited to invest in a fast-food franchise with several partners? Your research and professional advisors conclude that the offer is a well-structured venture, exactly the sort of break you need in order reach the next financial level.

Are you prepared? Do you have assets (not your three-month emergency fund or a credit card) to make the initial investment? A CD you can liquidate? Rental income? Investments that have doubled in value? If you own something, you probably do.

You must invest in yourself.

Opportunities are not always external. Maybe you need to make an investment in your own idea or talent. Perhaps your income is too high for your children to receive financial aid for college and you take on the responsibility of investing in them. You will sleep much better at night and actually look forward to the first of the month if you are able to use your assets to pay as you go, rather than dive deeply into dumb debt.

Student loans and mortgages are referred to as "smart debt" because they ultimately help you grow financially as long as you make your payments in full and on time each month. "Dumb debt" is racking up credit card charges on things you don't need with impulsive, emotional purchases. Money management expert Dave Ramsey teaches that "debt is the most aggressively marketed product in our culture today." Yes, debt is a product just like that Michael Kors purse in your closet. Resist the urge to splurge every payday, and you will be prepared with a stash of cash when presented with a real opportunity to make your George Washingtons (dollar bills) become Benjamin Franklins (hundred-dollar bills).

Owning something creates *transferable* wealth. What a head start! Families can literally lift themselves out of one financial class and into another by owning something and passing it to the next generation.

Clearly, these tips refer to things within your control. Sometimes natural disasters, illness, or sudden death can create horrific changes in your circumstances that no amount of planning can avert. Focus on the things you can anticipate and control. A final benefit of ownership and accumulating assets is that you are in a position to help those in need. The wonderful feeling of helping a friend or family member during a legitimate, unpredictable crisis is a better reward than any credit card company can offer.

MAKE FRIENDS WITH PEOPLE WHO INSPIRE YOU

When I was a very young, my parents insisted on knowing everything about a new friend before allowing me to have a sleepover at her house. Where does she live? Who are her parents? Does she make good grades? I thought all the cross-examination was major overkill. As an adult, parent, and grandparent, I now understand my parents were not being elitist. Instead, they were trying to ensure I spent my time in a safe environment with people who shared our principles. My closest friends today date back to those early friendships. They continue to inspire and encourage me.

*Cultivate relationships with
people who have similar goals to yours.*

Choosing a friend based on whether he or she has money is foolish, and shunning those facing financial difficulty is downright immoral. A person whose relationships are based solely on what potential gal pals have or what they can do for her is no friend worth having. Friends are like children, shoes, and careers: you are allowed to have more than one. Your friends probably span the financial spectrum. However, when trying to improve your financial situation, your job is to select acquaintances who encourage and educate you. Think of these folks as your financial friendship team and make sure to draft top players for the positions.

You need a friend who is your **financial peer**. Ideally, that is someone with the same financial means, responsibilities, and goals as yours. Parents who are struggling with putting their kids (or themselves) through college can relate to others who are going through the same thing. A young professional trying to succeed in a big city cannot construct a realistic budget based on advice from a friend who lives back home in a garage apartment or a brownstone on the Upper West Side of New York. Pair up with someone in a similar situation. In making your selection, the most important quality your financial peer must have is goals that complement yours.

You also need a friend who is your **financial superior**. Here is some advice from almost every woman's financial superior, Oprah Winfrey: "I still think twice before I buy anything." Good advice, right? Well, you probably have people in your network who have equally great wisdom to share. Go ahead. Ask them to be your financial mentor.

Finding this team member is tricky because you must separate your true financial superior from the bling blingers (BBs). One distinction is BBs like to flaunt their material possessions. They always wear the best, spend the most, and brag the loudest. Unfortunately, everything you see is everything they have. They don't need a safe because they are wearing all their assets. Here's another clue. Nothing exposes a financial faker like an emergency. Pay attention to how your friends handle unexpected things like minor damage to their homes, a trip to urgent care, temporary unemployment, or a seasonal downturn in their business. If a friend can't weather a brief storm without having to get a personal loan from friends or family, she may not be the right person for this position on your team.

Your true financial superior is comfortable in her tax bracket and does not feel the need to tell you how much she spent on everything she buys. In fact, she may often complain about the cost of things, yet, not so miraculously, all her needs are met. She has assets you will never see because they're not portable. Her age (or his age) is not particularly important. That's why, on average, the length of your credit history is only about 15 percent of your FICO (credit) score. The FICO puts a lot of weight on people's payment history and the amount of debt they have because those factors reflect how well they manage their money. Remember: it's not how much you make; it's how much you keep.

You need a friend who is a **financial professional**. I definitely believe people deserve to be paid for their expertise. So, expect to pay a professional for his or her expert advice. Never try to take advantage of your friends by seeking free advice (or babysitting) you'd have to pay for otherwise. By having a financial professional in your circle of friends, you will learn new things, almost by osmosis. Even a simple discussion of current events can help you better understand the economy or health care. We all have something to share; as long as you're willing to give as much as you get from the relationship, the friendship will grow like your FICO!

THE TAX ACCOUNTANT'S STORY
(AS TOLD TO DR. MOE)

My office conducts an annual "satisfaction" survey to gauge staff morale. One of the questions is "Do you have a best friend at work?" The question is hard for me because I have four or five people there who are friends for life. Janet, for instance, whose office is adjacent to mine, is someone I like a lot. Every morning we take a few minutes to talk about what is going on in the office, family happenings, and other stuff. Janet works part-time and is an SUV-driving, suburban mom with two college-age girls and one son in middle school. Most days, Janet brings her lunch. She dresses nicely, but is not a one-woman fashion show. I, on the other hand, drive a sedan, live in one of the most affluent zip codes in Texas, and go out to lunch more often than I brown-bag it.

Even so, I thought my financial stuff was pretty tight. Nice, reliable vehicle—paid for. Home—an appreciating investment. Money in the bank. Low debt. Then, over coffee one day, I found out that Janet is a trust-fund baby. I am not. Her children are trust-fund babies. No such thing in my family. Growing up, my sister and I enjoyed home-baked Easter ham at the kitchen table, complete with the Dole pineapples and cherries on top, while Janet and her sisters dined on a lavish buffet at their country club. These days, Janet's parents take their extended family—daughters, spouses, grandchildren—on vacation (Europe, anyone?) when the mood strikes them. My parents love my sister and me, but all trips taken by the Dansby girls are paid for by the Dansby girls. When the time came for Janet's daughters to go to college, quality of education came first, money second. My nephews and my step-daughter started out in junior colleges because they were not able to get scholarships and we couldn't pay their tuition in cash.

When I discovered that the money in Janet's family went back at least two generations, and saw the differences in how our families live, my friendship with Janet expanded to include talks about money. I immediately discovered that while I am quite good at saving money, I hadn't paid enough attention to generational planning. Tips from Janet inspired me to fund a trust for the young people in my family.

Our morning conversations now include discussion on Wall Street, mortgage rates, and retirement. Sometimes, she comes up with a bright idea about how we can make the most of our money, and sometimes I share a friendly financial tidbit. The relationship works well for both of us. So, if anyone ever asks whether I have a best *financial* friend at work, the answer is definitely yes.

LESSON SIX SUMMARY

☞ You don't get cash equity without providing sweat equity.

☞ Being smart about money now ensures a better future.

☞ Compare prices on every purchase and shop for the best deals on contracted services.

☞ Own something that appreciates in value over time.

☞ Ownership creates transferable wealth.

☞ Draft the best available players for your financial friendship team.

Lesson Seven:
Language Is a Tool, Not a Weapon

COMMUNICATION IS AN exchange of ideas with the purpose of building life-enriching relationships. In order to be a good leader, it is imperative to become an excellent communicator. Listening is key to this instruction, but don't limit your academic or professional pursuits to gathering information. Also, learn to deliver information in a way that informs and motivates others, regardless of their ages, cultures, or genders.

SHUT UP WITHOUT SHUTTING DOWN

Leadership is more than a title such as president or CEO or COO or supervisor. It is more than perks such as a company credit card or a suite at the local NBA franchise's arena. Leadership is demanding. You must formulate plans, organize, delegate, and supervise. Your main job is motivating others to work together toward a shared vision. If you don't have employees to supervise, you still plan, organize, delegate, and supervise your own activities, then you persuade others to invest in your vision.

I have worked with many great leaders, from COOs of large corporations to multimillion-dollar athletes. The one major thing they all have in common is something so simple and subtle it often is overlooked. Before I tell you what they have in common, I'll share what their common denominator is *not*.

The one thing these great leaders have in common is *not* an Ivy League education. Former Secretary of State Colin Powell, the first African-American chairman of the Joint Chiefs of Staff and the first African-American Secretary of State, graduated from City College of New York and earned his MBA at George Washington University. These are fine schools, but they do not have the prestigious reputation of some other institutions on the East Coast.

Another thing that great leaders do *not* necessarily have in common is a genius-level IQ. Some don't even come close. Out of diplomacy (and fear of retaliation), I'll refrain from giving examples. Just Google "stupid leaders." Seriously. Try it. Nor is it money that distinguishes the superior movers and shakers from the mediocre. Mother Teresa of Calcutta was born Gonxha (Agnes) Bojaxhu. She did not grow up poor, but she gave up affluence to become a nun and, later, to work with the poorest of the poor. It was as a poor nun that she was able to draw the attention of the entire world to suffering children in India simply with her dedication and tireless devotion.

What is it? What is the great, common denominator of these great, uncommon leaders? That's debatable, but I want to focus on the one that is absolutely, positively, not optional!

All good leaders are good listeners.

This is not a skill you inherit or purchase, but it is a skill that you absolutely must develop if you want to be a leader in your home, your profession, and your community. One of the keys to creating a rewarding relationship is what Dr. John Gray, of *Men Are from Mars* fame, calls "purposeful communication." He defines purposeful communication as communication with the intent to understand and be understood. This leads to loving, trusting, life-enriching relationships, as opposed to communication designed to manipulate, control, fault-find, embarrass, and disapprove. That kind of communication merely leads to resentment and anger.

Purposeful communication is heard and understood, and it has a positive emotional impact. It begins with listening.

Stephen R. Covey, author of the self-improvement classic *The Seven Habits of Highly Effective People* (1990, Free Press), says, "We listen at one of five levels": ignoring, pretend, selective, attentive, and empathic. Empathic listening is the ultimate level of listening. It means hearing and responding with both the heart and mind to understand the speaker's words, intent, and feelings. It is important to put yourself in the other person's shoes. Only if you understand the speaker's intent and feelings can you respond without bias and preconceived notions.

After listening, do not become defensive, try to solve the problem, or jump in with an opinion before you restate what the speaker has said and acknowledge his or her feelings. This is particularly important when dealing with someone who is upset. Try something like, "You have the right to feel angry. Let me make sure I understand the problem. You feel unappreciated because..."

*Take a vow of silence. Simply
stop talking and listen.*

Realize that the largest component of communication actually has nothing to do with your words. If you are essentially ignoring what another person is saying because your mind is preoccupied with something else or you're too busy thinking about your response, you will not connect in a positive manner. Even worse, your leadership abilities will not grow because you will not grow.

For practice, try taking a vow of silence during the next family or business meeting you attend. Don't say a word, no matter how ridiculous the conversation becomes. Listen as if you're going to be tested on the information. If you find this challenge very difficult or impossible, consider the possibility that you don't usually listen very well. I guarantee you'll hear something useful, something you wouldn't have heard if you were merely biding time until you could politely interrupt the speaker. You need new information and new ideas to feed your ravenous brain. How can you hear, except by listening with open eyes, open ears, and an open mind?

*Accept it. You don't know everything.
Listen and learn.*

(AFFIRM)ATIVE INTERACTION

Standard English is the universal dialect in America. Native and informal languages are not inferior to Standard English, but, generally, they are not the best choice for classrooms and boardrooms where your ultimate objective is to be understood. On the other hand, it is the highest order of ignorance and elitism to assume that someone who doesn't speak "good" English, or any English, is not intelligent and, therefore, unworthy of your respect. We tend to forget that millions of immigrants who came to this country during the colonial period did not speak English. They spoke a variety of languages, such as Spanish, Polish, Russian, Mende, German...In fact, many of the slaves brought to this country spoke multiple languages because they engaged in trade with Europeans while in Africa. Some slaves served as translators for their owners in the New World. Further, just because someone doesn't use the grammar of a person with advanced education doesn't mean he or she is not smart or wise.

Having multiple skills at work provides job security. Speaking multiple languages gives you both corporate and social/cultural capital everywhere. As the advance of technology makes everyone your neighbor, I encourage you who have mastered English to spend less time judging those who haven't and more time learning another language.

Don't forget, good leaders are also tolerant. Are you sometimes too quick to judge others by subjective standards? For instance, do you immediately frown when you hear a foreign accent in the voice of the person answering your call for customer support? Are you frowning because you think he or she took a job away from some "real" American, or because you anticipate communication difficulties, or is it because the person is not like you? Think about the biases you may unconsciously harbor and work to overcome them.

When it's your turn to talk:

Be precise and specific in your communication. Get to the point with a few words that have a few syllables. Sometimes those of us with a couple of letters before or behind our names get carried away with the mellifluous sound of our own voices. You know, the ones in class or at the staff meeting who go on and on about nothing for half an hour, wasting time, ticking everybody off. In addition to criticizing them in the break room or texting *during* the meeting, make a mental note not to emulate their behavior.

There is nothing wrong with being well educated or utilizing the full extent of your professional lexicon or personal idiolect. But what is the point of using big words, if it sounds like German to your American English–speaking audience? There is a time and a place to use words like *panopticon*. Most of the time and in most places, listeners prefer to hear a brief, vivid discussion of the circular-shaped prison with the guard's desk in the center than a bland, boring monologue about the *panopticon*. If you really want to be loved, needed, and necessary, say what you mean, mean what you say, and then sit down to thunderous applause from appreciative listeners.

....

Impact others and become an agent for change with
common language and **uncommon** *conviction.*

....

The comfort of a shared experience or background, where the bonds are so strong that words are not necessary, is incomparable. Being with people who know us, understand us, and are like us helps keep our sense of identity. We know "one of us" by the voice inflection, attire, eyes, or skin tone. Countless sensory cues, linked to our survival instincts, also let us know when someone is *different*, and we may feel threatened or uncomfortable.

Fortunately, we have evolved beyond our basic survival instincts. A better approach than fleeing or fighting is seeking commonalities, asking a few questions like, "Is this other person really different from me?" and "What exactly am I afraid of?" The threat is often as imaginary as a character in a Disney movie. If we each practice a little more tolerance, race relations in America will stop being a topic of discussion.

Consider this scenario: you have a coworker who, like you, is a wife, mother, and civic volunteer. Two peas in the same pod, right?

Maybe. Maybe not. What if, aside from knowing that your coworker is a wife and mom, all you know about her is that she is a first generation immigrant with a heavy accent? Pronouncing her name correctly is challenging for you, and your tastes in food are vastly different. These things might lead you to assume that the two of you could never be friends. Based on your assumption, you categorize your coworker, put her in a "hidden folder," and password protect her file in your mind. You don't really think she's stupid or treat her dismissively; you simply do not try to get to know her. The closest you ever get to her is sitting by her at a conference table or perhaps sharing a ride to an off-site meeting, but that doesn't make her your friend. And because you don't try, you never learn that you and your coworker both enjoy playing Farmville, going scuba diving, watching the Cooking Channel, and collecting unusual paper clips. In fact, you may have more in common with her than you do with members of your own family...who look exactly like you.

We must avoid letting minor differences impede our ability to communicate effectively, making any shared mission or endeavor much less effective. Great leaders are flexible and tolerant enough to work with people who do not agree with all of their beliefs.

As I write these words, the world is mourning the death of South African President Nelson Mandela. During the memorial service for Mandela, President Barack Obama shook hands with Raul Castro, the leader of the Cuban Communist Party. It caused quite a stir in the blogosphere, similar to what was written when President Richard Nixon shared a robust handshake with Chinese communist dictator Mao Tse Tung during a visit to China in 1972. The question is, do we actually expect world leaders to snub one another at diplomatic events that are televised around the world? A handshake does not equal a change of protocol or policy, nor does a greeting from you to someone you don't understand make you a weak person. It takes much more strength of character to exceed the low standards set by your natural instincts than it does to be rude. Ultimately, our actions say much more about us than any words.

It is imperative that we all think and act cooperatively with the very best minds available in order to reach our full potential.

We cannot be afraid to step out and affirmatively pursue cross-cultural, personal, and business relationships, even when it makes us uncomfortable.

How do you get rid of those little voices in your head that are still telling you to avoid strangers, fifteen years after your parents stopped issuing that warning? Do a little antibrainwashing to get rid of the notion that other people have to look like you or think like you in order to be valued friends, associates, or sources of information. If you've decided to take the initiative on expanding your relationships and your world view, don't let cosmetic differences stop you.

THE PROBLEM WITH CHEERLEADING

The challenge in communicating with the opposite sex, whether it is with your son or your spouse, is often the different ways in which we are socialized. We all emerge from the womb completely self-centered. We are taught how to successfully interact with others by respecting their wants and needs. In America, however, the lessons are usually somewhat different for males and females.

Does this sound familiar? Around the ages of twelve to fourteen, many girls become "cheerleaders" instead of the players. By that, I mean they give up conflict and go with peer pressure. They learn to giggle and gossip. On the other hand, most boys in this age group become more competitive, more performance driven, and less judgmental.

Visit your local park and observe the interactions. Most of the boys are playing soccer or basketball, and most of the girls are in small groups laughing and talking. If two girls argue, the activity stops and everyone expresses their opinion about who was at fault. If two boys fight, the other boys break it up and the game continues. In essence, the girls bond through emotions and the boys bond through events.

The girls emphasize compromise, sensitivity, communication, and cooperation. The boys emphasize negotiating, confidence, winning, and roles. When boys choose teams, they select the fastest, tallest, and strongest player available, even if they don't like him. The other boys may feel bad about not being picked, but they don't take offense. They do push-ups and drink protein shakes to get stronger and better, turning their energy inward. Girls usually pick their best friend, even if she sucks at the game, and they may even say mean things about the girls who were not picked, focusing their energy outward. These learned habits sometimes stay with us for a lifetime.

As we grow up, we must discard old, bad habits. If silence hasn't worked in the past five relationships, it's time to speak up. If letting someone else take the credit means you get passed over for another promotion, it's time to speak up. Moving ahead in life means committing to reaching the "goal line," and you cannot do that from the sideline.

There's an old adage, "Chase your dreams." Great advice if you don't delete the adjective "your." Too many of us who do suit up and play end up chasing everyone's dreams but our own. Boyfriend's dreams...parents' dreams...corporate vision...images created by, for, and about someone else. The directive "to chase" indicates the dreams are separate from us and somehow beyond our control. So we chase them and hope they are not too elusive for capture.

Actually, what we should do is *carry* our dreams everywhere we go instead of setting them down to chase others' goals. Sometimes we put them away and stray so far from them for so long that we forget where we placed our hopes for safekeeping. If you must make that sacrifice to help someone, run back and touch your own dreams as often as possible. Take some small action to move them every month: an inch or a mile closer to becoming reality. Remember, however, that good friends and loved ones will do the same for you when they are able.

LIFELINE

I have two sons, now in their twenties. I have so many wonderful memories of their childhoods. It was a learning experience for them and me. I grew up with a younger sister and the ways of men were, and continue to be, a mystery to me. I'll never forget a conversation I overheard my younger son having when he was about eight years old.

My baby boy told his buddy, "Clifton is the fastest kid in my class. I'm third fastest when Eddie is absent, but if he's in the race, then I'm fourth fastest."

His friend Josh responded proudly, "I'm the second fastest slow kid in my class."

I did a double take. "What did you say Josh?" I asked, laughing. "Did you say that you're the second fastest slow kid?"

"Yes, ma'am. I'm not a very good runner. I can't beat any of the fast kids like Clifton, but if a bunch of us slow kids race, I'm second-best!"

Josh said those words with such confidence. His oval face glowed with pride because he was near the top of the bottom of the racing barrel. I can't even imagine myself saying that I am the second prettiest, fairly average-looking chick in my social circle. Even if I thought that, and I do have some beautiful friends, there is no way I would utter those words in public. I will stand in my bathroom mirror and pick my body apart like a vulture, but if I do that out loud, someone might agree with me. And then, what will I do?

Ladies, can you visualize your partner saying that he's the third-best son-in-law in the family? No way, not gonna happen. I don't care how much money your sister's partner makes or how many diapers he changes.

That's not a problem. By the time you reach middle age, so many other people are finding fault with you that it's understandable if you don't want to join the chorus. Kids, on the other hand, just don't have all these issues.

I felt bad for poor, slow Josh, so I said, "Next year, Clifton and a lot of the other boys will go to a different school and then maybe you'll be one of the fastest kids."

Josh looked horrified at my suggestion. "I hope we get more fast kids from some of the other elementary schools or we won't have a good football team."

"Josh, if you work out this summer and eat healthy foods, you could get faster," I persisted.

"Nope," he assured me. "My Mom and Dad are slow as cold ketchup. I'm always gonna be slow."

It's hard to argue with genetics. "I bet you're really good at some other things, Josh," I said hopefully.

Josh piped up immediately, "I'm the best pencil sharpener in my class."

Well, there's something to be proud of. Though I wonder how that has worked out for him in this digital age?

Subsequent to the passage of Title IX of the Education Amendments in 1972 and other antidiscrimination laws, girls are taking a different view of competitive sports. However, feelings are still a major factor in the decision processes of girls and women.

Why is it important to understand our American socialization process?

Though no one likes to emphasize or generalize about gender differences, there are undeniable patterns of behavior we must examine and understand, or when necessary, dissect and change in order to become more effective leaders.

Those boys from the playground become men who give orders and focus on activities and skills rather than building consensus. They like to give advice and solve problems. Men hear about a problem and they offer a solution. "If you hate your job, just quit." There's nothing to talk about. Comedian Wanda Sykes quips, "Men like sports so much because they don't have to think and talk a lot. If there's a dispute, the referee decides, and it's over. Play ball!"

Most women, however, are socially conditioned to discuss things and share. We want details and feelings. Dr. Deborah Tannen calls it "matching troubles." You tell your friend about something awful that happened at work, and she tells you about something awful that happened to her. You don't need her to fix it. You want her to empathize and understand.

Women have the reputation for being avid talkers, but that only applies in private. In public, several studies have proven that men tend to dominate the conversations. They usually ask the first and longest questions at meetings. They interrupt the speaker or their coworkers more frequently. They have learned this is the way to get attention and respect at work. At home? Not so much.

On the other hand, many women believe they should explain their requests, instead of simply giving orders. We will solicit feedback (aka buy-in) from everyone likely to be impacted before making a decision. We were getting input from stakeholders long before they coined a phrase for the practice. For us, conversation is a way to build relationships both at work and at home.

Here are a few tips about both sexes that apply at home and in the workplace. (Warning: generalizations used to illustrate a point. If it doesn't apply to you, that's okay.)

1. **Women like details.** We are going to ask questions and we want men to ask questions about what we're saying. That is how we know they're listening to us. Nodding or saying "uh-huh" from behind the newspaper is not enough. If that's what he's doing and it bothers you, tell him. And tell him why.

2. Ladies, if you're giving a presentation and a male member of the audience challenges something you've said, you must **be prepared to defend your position.** It's not personal. This is usually more a sign of respect or curiosity than it is condescension.

3. **Women have a tendency to phrase ideas as questions.** "Don't you think? Or "What if?" Be assertive. Speak up in a strong voice and make statements supported with facts when necessary. Be confident. If someone interrupts you (other than your boss), do not, I repeat, do not stop talking. Make the other person wait for his or her turn to speak.

4. **Women enjoy direct eye contact.** We sit or stand across from each other. We look at each other when we talk. Men sit with a chair between them whenever possible and look around a lot when they're talking. If you're trying to make a good impression, you need to mirror the style of the person you're talking to, but never stare. That's just weird and frightening.

5. **Women often react differently to stress.** Men may shut down. They need time to process what's happened. They don't want to talk. Respect this emotional reaction and give them time and space. Conversely, women need to talk about an experience, and we often cry. Crying is not a sign of weakness. When we're upset, some of our hormones, such as prolactin, fluctuate, and that stimulates tear production just as aerobics produces perspiration. Additionally, the tear glands in a woman develop differently than they do in guys. Did you know that men actually have larger tear glands so they can hold more in before they spill over? It's not that they don't want to cry, but they have been taught not to cry, and they have more

time to get themselves together. Please recognize that crying doesn't mean we're hysterical or unable to think clearly. It means **nothing** except that our natural design makes us more likely to cry when we experience the same emotional stimulus as a man. Girlfriends, dry your eyes, blow your nose, and keep talking. Don't run to the bathroom. Don't apologize for crying. Find a sympathetic face to give you positive eye contact and just keep talking. You'll recover and your voice will get stronger as you go on.

....

Crying is **not** *a sign of weakness.*

....

LESSON SEVEN SUMMARY

☞ *All* leaders are good listeners.

☞ Strive to improve your ability to listen purposefully.

☞ Occasionally, take a vow of silence and practice listening.

☞ Use common language and uncommon conviction to express your ideas.

☞ Pursue cross-cultural relationships.

☞ Don't stop talking when a man interrupts you, unless you have finished.

☞ Crying is physiological. It is not a sign of weakness.

Lesson Eight:
Rule Your Queendom

VIEW EVERY POSITION you attain, whether at the office, in the community, at temple/church...even as the matriarch of the family as a position of relevance and influence. Never allow your circumstances, particularly when they are less than ideal, to deceive you into thinking your life is not in your control. Every decision, even a decision to do nothing, has potent repercussions. We are all self-governing, with influence over our destinies.

Always act from a position of power, not fear.

FAKE IT 'TIL YOU MAKE IT

Any woman who projects confidence even when she feels unqualified and anxious, is an example of how you Fake It 'Til You Make It. From the way they walked with their heads erect and eyes forward, to the way they maintained piercing eye contact while speaking, pioneering women such as the suffragettes, who fought for American women's right to vote, always appeared to be in control

My mother is a retired principal and an ordained minister. The joke goes that she "drugged me as a child." I was drug to Camp Fire Girl meetings. I was drug to piano lessons, and I was drug to church two or three times a week. At countless church programs, I was given the assignment of standing in front of hundreds of adults to make a speech or give an announcement. It didn't matter how I felt about it. No one rescued me or the other "suffragettes" if our knees shook, voices quivered, or we forgot our lines. It was big girl boot camp in the neighborhood, a rite of passage, if you will. The leading ladies of our lives hovered nearby, smiling encouragement while insisting we finish what we started. And eventually, we all gained the confidence to keep calm and carry on.

Maybe you don't have a late-model car, designer clothing, a thousand-dollar watch, or other material things that announce you have "arrived." Perhaps it took seven years to earn your degree at the local community college. Annnnnd? Don't let a lack of status symbols cause you to feel inadequate and hinder your ability to take advantage of great opportunities.

For example, you spy the CEO at a boring company reception, standing alone with a friendly smile on her face. You've been waiting six months for a chance to introduce yourself and share a great idea that could increase the company's profits. Your supervisor won't listen to you, or he always takes credit for your ideas. What do you do? Seize the opportunity to go around that roadblock in a politically correct maneuver. Do not allow those negative voices in your head to chide, "Loser. She won't talk to you. You don't have a gargantuan class ring from her college alma mater. You get your hair cut at the mall with a coupon. This suit is four years old. And your idea sucks."

When the naysayers in your mind start casting stones, remember you're a queen. Do you really think a queen would let someone talk to her like that? The voices in your head are under your control, subject to your rules. Shut them up. Bring new, supportive, encouraging advisors out of your subconscious. Affirm yourself and make something positive happen in your kingdom. Unless you're a professional athlete or entertainer, it's unlikely anyone is going to go out of their way to tell you how wonderful you are today and every day. Tell your damn self! Only in fairy tales do mirrors assure someone they are the fairest of them all.

IN-courage! Find the strength from within to excel.

Impossible, you think. I can't do it. If you occasionally struggle with low self-confidence, another way to fake it 'til you make it is by emulating someone you admire. If you have a loudmouth, fearless friend, pretend to be her when you need courage. Be her with class and good grammar, but be her. If you have a level-headed, rational friend, be her when you see your man out on a date with your BFF...in your car! Be your spiritual friend from church when you must console someone who is grieving. Ask yourself, "What would (insert role model's name) say/do under these circumstances?"

In time, you will find you don't need to ask yourself this question because your ongoing efforts to improve your position in life will transform you into a person with boldness, patience, compassion, loyalty, or whatever good qualities you seek to develop further.

EAT LUNCH WITH STRANGERS

As the saying goes, if you always do what you've always done, you'll always be what you've always been. Nowhere is that more true than in the workplace. Venture beyond the familiar if you truly want your life to grow in a new dimension. That is more than a new course. You can walk backward and call it a new course, but it doesn't get you any closer to your objectives. A new dimension implies growth in every direction, elevating you to a new level of influence.

One trap many wanna-be executives get stuck in is becoming part of a clique. It is in your best interest to have friends at work, but usually your friends are in the same position you're in and they don't have information that will help get you promoted. Talk to them before and after work. Not during work. Be on the job for your employer and yourself. That means your communication and action on the job should be productive. Gossiping about someone in another department is not productive. Eating lunch with someone from the marketing department or having coffee with the VP's administrative assistant is productive. Do not pry them for confidential information. Do not take this as an opportunity to lodge your complaints. Simply be pleasant. Make a good impression. Listen. Don't just ask what they do; ask them why. That question will elicit a very different response.

Show genuine interest in the other person. In fact, don't talk much at all. People love to talk about themselves. Allow them to do so. You can never make too many good impressions. Be kind and professional to everyone you encounter, not just people you think are in a position to further your cause. You cannot have too many people who know your name and think you're an asset to the company.

As often as possible, eat lunch with new people. It's a great way to see the world through another person's lens and build your network at the same time.

LIFELINE

I transferred from the University of Texas at Houston School of Dentistry to the University of Minnesota School of Dentistry after my first year of professional school. The school in Houston had about a dozen African-American students in each class. The school in Minnesota had one African-American student—in the entire dental school. He was a senior when I arrived and doubled the African-American enrollment. Though I'd always attended integrated schools, this was the culture shock of my life. Not only was I the only African-American in my class of about a hundred, but I was also the only Baptist, the only person from the South, and, later, the only person in my class to have a baby smack dab in the middle of a semester. (Yes, it was planned. I don't know what I was thinking.) Add to that laundry list the fact that I was married and lived in the suburbs while most of my classmates were single and lived near the University of Minnesota campus in Minneapolis.

I couldn't have been more different than everyone if I'd fallen from a spaceship.

Dental school is more like elementary school than college in that everyone in your class takes the same courses at the same time. There is no night school or five-year program, which is why I missed less than two weeks after my nine-pound son, Tony, was born. There is one instructor per subject. You never ask anyone, "What is your schedule?" or "How many hours are you taking?" My classmates were together eight plus grueling hours a day, five days a week, for one year before I arrived. They were already friends with cliques and had memories that did not include me.

On my first day, I remember going into a huge lecture room and finding a seat near the middle of the room. I was one of the first to arrive. Slowly, my new classmates trickled in, laughing and recounting their summer vacations. They exchanged greetings and hugs. They sat in clusters around me and looked at me curiously as if I were a new black sun in their otherwise familiar universe. The instructor was running late. This gave everyone even more time to unintentionally make me feel like a special project at the science fair. It wasn't their action but their lack of action that made me feel so isolated. Eventually, one brave soul, Kierian, the class president, walked over and introduced himself. Later, during lunch, a group of female students invited me to join them. I hesitated. I almost declined because I was so stressed from trying to fake it 'til I made it home and had a good I-can't-do-this-I-wanna-go-back-to-Texas cry. But a dormant voice in my mind said, "Go on and play with the other kids. It might be fun." So I did, and I made a lot of new friends.

After that, I ate lunch with whomever invited me, and yes, often, but not exclusively, it was the same group of women. I learned about Elena's escape from the former Soviet Union and Todd's experience playing on the gold-medal-winning US soccer team. Kierian's wife was a nurse, and Karen had two sons. Jan had a gift of encouragement, and Nancy always made me laugh. Dr. Jean Merry and I were pregnant at the same time. I joined her family practice after I graduated.

Well, the story ends three years later when I stood on the stage at commencement and gave the address as senior class president. I was elected to this position by my classmates. There is no way I would have been elected if I had let our differences make me feel uneasy. I didn't dwell on our differences. I constantly reminded myself of our common interest, which was a desire to become health care professionals, helping others. We worked together to reach our goals, and that became possible when one person extended a hand of friendship and I was brave enough to take it.

MAN UP!

Talk show host and comedian Steve Harvey told us all to act like a lady, think like a man in his bestselling book on the subject of how men really feel about relationships and commitment. I solved some perplexing mysteries from my past using his insights. What I'll add to that conversation is that sometimes ladies need to be a little less Southern Belle and a lot more give-'em-hell.

Today's metrosexual man is quick to let a woman know he is in touch with his X chromosome. But—when was the last time you heard a female brag about tapping into her natural testosterone?

(Seriously, women *do* have testosterone. See http://women.webmd. com/normal-testosterone-and-estrogen-levels-in-women.)

When women first entered the workplace alongside men, we masked our differences, trying to fit into the male-dominated work place. We tried hard to avoid those horrid stereotypical labels that they give to women who actually act like, well, women. Those in the corporate world wore conservative black and navy suits with clunky two-inch heels, for example, as if they were going to a funeral every single day. Now that women are an accepted part of the work force (more or less), the pendulum has swung the other way, and we strive to express our true selves, our femininity, even at work. Thank goodness, we have CEOs such as Marissa Mayer, current head of Yahoo, posing on the cover of *Vogue* magazine. Some reacted with horror, but I applaud her ability to pull off chic geek while (to date) reversing the fortunes of that global company. She was several months pregnant when she got the promotion to CEO, by the way.

Sure, act like a lady, but when it comes to how you permit others to treat you, don't just think like a man, *act* like one, too. There are some traits associated with strong men that I recommend emulating during tough times. Do not hide and cower, waiting for the dark knight to defend you. Do not let down your hair, hoping someone will climb your hair extensions to rescue you. They probably can't support a man's weight anyway. And do not lie in your bed crying and hoping things will get better by some miracle. Man up, and switch from defensive to offensive against whomever or whatever poses a legitimate threat to your welfare. For example, if you are a victim of sexual harassment, understand that is a form of sexual discrimination per the Civil Rights Act of 1964. In the past, we shrugged off this type of behavior because we were conditioned to believe "boys will be boys." Well, those boys need to become men who treat their female colleagues in a professional manner at all times just as they would want someone to treat their mothers, sisters, or wives.

You have numerous options for seeking a resolution, including trying direct communication or third-party mediation, reporting the behavior to a supervisor/the authorities, and involving human resources. That works in some cases with some people. Research and reality TV have demonstrated that some folks simply cannot be reasoned with no matter how skillfully you try. Then, you need to reassess your strategic plan and counter the attack.

....
Your enemies should fear what you might *do.*
....

Discuss the situation and your feelings with an unbiased witness. Perhaps you're way off base. If there is no doubt, then man up. Sometimes, ironically, that means a new job or new neighborhood for you, not them. That is not considered retreating in defeat unless you leave without taking action. A legitimate complaint to the planning and zoning department or an honest exit interview is a form of paying it forward. How will things ever change if no one speaks up? Do you want to go to your next job and work for a manager who has been groping his direct reports for ten years with impunity? Please do not leave that bad situation unchanged for the next person, or the glass ceiling will become a glass floor we all fall through.

ANGEL'S STORY

Angel recently had the horrible experience of being accused of theft of time—think sneaking off to the movies in the middle of the day. She was summarily fired and threatened with criminal prosecution. Angel fell apart, but her best friend propped her up and insisted that she fight back against the false allegations. She could have proven that she was actually meeting with a client during her absence if anyone had bothered to ask. She appealed to human resources and got her job back, along with a nice apology from the company. The person who made the false report was notorious for her two-hour lunches and early departures. When Angel was rehired, her first order of business should have been to bring her adversary's attendance record to the attention of their supervisor. Angel decided to "turn the other cheek and be a bigger person." Never mind that Angel's nemesis never offered an apology and continued to malign her reputation with false gossip. To this day, Angel cries on her way to work and cries on her way home. Luckily, she only has three more years of crying before she can retire.

No one should be as miserable as Angel. To get rid of a weed, ladies, kill the root. I'll take some heat for this chapter, but I'll be willing to roast if it means one of you will not have to go through the sad ordeals that Angel and I and millions of other women have endured in the past because we didn't fight back when necessary. This advice does not apply to someone with a bad attitude or someone having a bad day. You should ignore that temporary condition. This last-resort admonition is only for vicious, vindictive people with a pattern of destructive behavior. For them, and only for them, document everything and include witnesses. Prepare your case until you have so much dirt on your enemy, the Pope would fire him or her. This process will also help you determine if you are wrong, because your files will be woefully thin and circumstantial if you are reading the situation incorrectly. Be patient like an animal in the wild. You don't have to lie, just lie in wait. Never turn the other cheek when your welfare is threatened.

....

Don't lie. Do lie in wait.

....

Do not yield your territory easily, and certainly not without a fight. When you come up with a good idea at work and another team member takes credit for it, he or she is encroaching on your intellectual property. If your teenage daughter speaks to with you with folded arms and open contempt, she is crapping all over your turf. And if a woman is bold enough to call your man on his cell at eleven o'clock at night, and he has the nerve to answer, well... The common thread in these circumstances is they require a response that, at the least, will be uncomfortable and could escalate. Knowing that things might get ugly, you still have to man up, put on your protective emotional gear, and confront the interloper. You never lose control of your mind or body. You don't have to yell or hit anyone to make a strong point. Remember, losing control of your emotions is a barrier to power. However, if you do not firmly and quickly address the trespass, it will happen again. You will suffer until you let it be known you have boundaries that are not to be crossed without consequences.

"Can't we all just get along?" Rodney King may have uttered the words, but women made the practice an art long before Rodney asked his infamous question. Most of us think if everyone sits down and calmly, laboriously, mind-numbingly talks it out, any conflict can be resolved. Our instinct is to fix a problem where we find it, even if the problem is not ours. The only time a woman is allowed to say, "That's not my problem" is when she's working a customer service job for which she is paid to solve problems. Other than that, women collect problems like black pumps and silver earrings.

Unlike my recommended reaction regarding a personal or professional threat, when it comes to solving everyone else's issues, we should master the art of letting it be.

Why should a woman pass on solving a problem if it is within her power to help? There are plenty of good reasons, but I'll focus on the main two. First, letting it be conserves energy. Time spent concentrating on others' issues, especially at work, is time taken away from your own responsibilities. And, if you are the typical working woman (at home or the office), you could probably use more time to attend to your own affairs. At work, you have a job description. "Other duties as assigned" does not mean you must play the role of mom, grandma, or the wise auntie who has a ready answer for every dilemma, nor should you want to be. Do the work you are paid to do. Psychologists are paid to help people with their problems. Make the appropriate referral and get back to handling your own business.

Which brings us to the second reason for letting it be: you are not necessarily doing a good deed by solving another person's problems. All you do is make the person overly dependent on you or your replacement. As a rule, we do not like it when our loved ones are having a difficult time with life lessons. But, as the saying goes, life is a series of lessons, and we repeat the same lesson until we master it. No one can learn to hold a job, delay gratification, or generally navigate through life if you keep hovering over him or her like a SWAT team in a helicopter. You can be the safety net, but (sometimes) you've got to let others walk the tightrope. Tap into your girly testosterone and tamp down the urge to rescue others who will be stronger and more resourceful once they learn to help themselves.

Go ahead. Be yourself. Walk like a girl. Throw like a girl. Eat like a girl. From tomboy to prom queen, be the woman you are by nature. But when it comes to personal security threats, at times you must act like a man. Your great idea or world's best home-based business means nothing if you are not prepared to defend it.

....

Do not back down when you're right.
Don't be humble. Don't waver.

....

PAY THE TAXES ON YOUR TITLE

Nothing ruins a night out with friends quite like Frankie the Freeloader. She orders the most expensive item on the menu and treats the wait staff as if they are slightly less than human beings.

She sends her food back once, her drink back twice, and complains continuously about the poor service. When the bill comes, Frankie offers twenty dollars for her meal, tax, and tip toward her fifty-dollar tab. Eyes roll, stilettos tap beneath the table, but no one says a word. Everyone works hard, and Frankie actually earns more than half the members of the group, yet she refuses to pay her fair share. Otherwise, Frankie's girlfriend credentials are pretty good. She's witty, intelligent, loyal, and a good listener, but because she leaves it up to others to cover what she ought to willingly chip in, Frankie will soon be deleted from the First Friday's dinner list. Both sides suffer the loss. The friends will miss Frankie's funny quips, and Frankie will miss the camaraderie, all because she refuses to pay the taxes on the dividends of friendship.

Apply Frankie's story to your professional life. Like her, you have the basics covered. Your automatic reinvestments in your personal development have paid off with a position that allows you some financial flexibility. With that "gain" comes extras dues or "taxes," if you will, that you are expected to pay on your good fortune. The good news about these taxes is that the payment does not have to be in cash, and it is not all due on April 15th. It can be made in whatever form you like, throughout the year. The tax I am referring to is service and philanthropy. You need to be involved in your professional and civic communities with both your time and resources to build your social capital.

Maybe you are thinking, "I've paid my dues. I don't owe anybody anything." Remember, no matter how much or how little you feel like you owe, the truth is, to reign in the world place, you absolutely must step out of your cubicle and share your gifts with your community. There's a reason there are over 1.5 million nonprofit organizations in the United States. Bill and Melinda Gates don't take donations from the public for their foundation, which has donated billions to various causes around the world. The Gateses are almost as well known for their foundation as they are for Microsoft, which Bill cofounded.

If your climb up the ladder of success moves you to the corner office where optional luxuries won't strain the monthly budget, go ahead, hire a housekeeper or lawn care service. Anything you can do to free your mind and time for more productive endeavors will benefit you and your family. Those who are active in professional associations receive goodwill returns such as referrals, advice, education, and lifelong friendships. Everyone knows a lot of positive networking happens where people come together, whether it is at an elite $10,000-a-plate fundraiser for the arts or at a neighborhood civic association's $10 all-you-can-eat barbeque. Get out and about, often. Pretend you're going to the bank to make a deposit every time you attend a meeting. Ultimately, you are making a difference in your future, your family's future, and the future of your community.

When you prepare your professional budget, include the taxes on your title!

CONGRESSWOMAN SHEILA JACKSON LEE

The US Representative for Texas's Eighteenth Congressional District is Sheila Jackson Lee. Her career is a primer in paying taxes on your title. Ever heard the phrase "meteoric rise" to the top? Lee's ascension was exactly the opposite. Her "title" when she moved to Houston included an undergraduate degree from Yale, a law degree, and a position at one of the city's top law firms. You might be impressed, but Houston's movers and shakers were not, because she was not a Houstonian—she was a Yankee from New York, for goodness sake—and she was not an alumna of one of Texas's historic colleges. Lee found herself in the top tax bracket when it came to the need to pay taxes on her title.

Lee immediately became active in several professional and civic organizations, and eventually she ran for a judgeship—and lost. Undaunted, she ran again and again and *lost*. Determined to make a positive impact, she did not let her setbacks deter her; she remained active and eventually received a municipal court judge appointment. That's traffic court, girls—not exactly the type of judicial post she envisioned with her Ivy League resume, but she took it and worked hard. She began networking with everybody, and I mean *everybody* in Houston. After work, she went to community meetings. On weekends, she attended birthday parties, weddings, even funerals. If you invited her to give a speech at a banquet for five, she showed up and spoke passionately as if she had an audience of five hundred.

When Congressman Mickey Leland died in a plane crash in 1989, the political fallout from the tragedy changed Houston's political landscape and Lee's destiny. Being the perennial loser of local contests, she was in no position to run for Congress. Two better-known, seasoned candidates campaigned for Leland's Eighteenth Congressional District seat. The good news for Lee was that one of the would-be Congressmen vacated his city council seat to campaign. Hmmm, take a guess who was poised and positioned to claim it?

In less than a decade, Councilmember Lee worked her way to the big time: a Congressional seat in Washington. She could have remained in her DC office, admiring the plaques on her wall and laughing at her haters, but that is not how a real leader remains engaged with the community. Instead, Lee continued to make appearances all over the local scene back home in Texas, and she was, without exception, accessible to the average Houstonian.

Now a household name to policy makers throughout the country; she travels around the world, but she still pays her taxes at home and makes her rounds in the neighborhoods. Cynical types find her omnipresence amusing, but consider this true story: A hair stylist excitedly told her client, "Shelia Jackson Lee came to our hair show." The client said something sarcastic about Sheila barging in and hogging the mic. "We didn't look at it that way," the stylist replied. "She told us about issues we needed to know about." Then, the client reflected and said, "You're right. No one ever talks to us until election time."

Footnote: perhaps you recall the stylishly dressed member of Congress who spoke at Michael Jackson's public tribute. You can be certain that's a speaking engagement many members of Congress would have gladly taken, considering the millions of viewers around the world who watched those proceedings on television and the Internet. Yet, it was Congresswoman Lee who got the coveted moment in the world's spotlight. Luck is when opportunity meets preparation.

WORK TOO HARD

You hear it all the time, maybe as you enter your office building on a Monday morning or head back to your work area after a fifteen-minute break: "Don't work too hard." The phrase is another way of saying "See you later," but isn't it really more than a simple good-bye? The words are a warning. *Don't work too hard.* What does it mean? What awful things might happen to those who work too hard? Will they be demoted or fired? Will they actually make less money?

Who has the answers? The unemployed?

Take pride in your work and invest in your career.

If you ask an entrepreneur whether or not "don't work too hard" is good advice, be prepared to duck. People who do not get a paycheck deposited directly in their bank accounts every other week, come rain or shine, don't comprehend the fairy-tale dream of reward without effort. Success belongs to those who hit it, and hit it hard, every dayum day. For entrepreneurs, the idea of not working hard makes no sense. After all, everybody knows that a woman in business for herself has to be willing to do more; in fact, we expect her to give at least 150 percent to her business. The same attitude is not necessarily true for those who are employees, rather than the boss.

It is almost impossible to work hard and not learn something new in the process. And guess what: the new things you learn belong exclusively to you, can't be taken from you, and go wherever you go. As American gymnast and Olympic Gold Medalist Mary Lou Retton puts it, "Working hard becomes a habit, a serious kind of fun."

How does a person who has fallen into the "don't work too hard" rut get out? First, put it at the front of your mind that every time you "hide" from work, you're actually dodging knowledge and opportunity. If you have to, play a mind trick on yourself: think of challenging assignments as you would a new hobby that requires dedication and a sharp mind. It might sound corny, but it works. If you are a singer, it might be daunting to take on a new solo, but because it's something you love, you don't mind working hard for a great performance. Think of your work, or the results of it, as something you benefit from personally, and it will seem a lot less like a prison sentence.

If that doesn't rev your engine, calculate exactly how much you make an hour and think about which bill you'll pay with the next hour of labor. In fact, keep bills in your purse and glance at them every time you get ready to quit or tell your employer to "take this job and shove it!" Once the bills are paid, start thinking about your vacation. "My eight hours today are paying for that long weekend with the family at the beach. Come on, five o'clock. Mama needs a new beach towel/botox/bedroom set."

Once you start working as if you're getting paid more than you are to do it, be prepared for your peers to complain. "Girl, I don't know what you're working so hard for. These people don't care about you." Or, "You have a 'good government job'; you don't have to work hard." Tee hee. Wink, wink. It's not funny. These taunts that are intended to make you lower your standards are on par with the kids who make Ds accusing the kids who make As of being nerds. If you find yourself in this situation, you know what to do. Start having lunch with strangers who also have a good work ethic.

No one is saying stress yourself out by working absurdly long hours, to the neglect of the other important areas of your life, such as your health or loved ones. Working hard is not being the last one to leave the office or the last one to go to bed every night. That may indicate you are not using your time efficiently or you are trying to do too much. It means putting forth your best effort for yourself and your employer even when no one is looking.

LESSON EIGHT SUMMARY

☞ Operate from a mind-set of power, not dread.

☞ Always appear to be prepared and in control even when you're not.

☞ Affirm yourself! IN-courage.

☞ New ideas come from new things, new people, and new places.

☞ Eat lunch with someone you don't know well at least once a month.

☞ Your enemies should fear you.

☞ You are your own advertising agency. Market yourself well.

☞ Pay the taxes on your title. Get involved in your community.

☞ You can work too long but never too hard.

Lesson Nine:
Schedule Your Nervous Breakdowns

WE SCHEDULE EVERYTHING these days. We schedule appointments, meetings, events, activities, and other to-dos up the woo hoo. Yet, none of these things get done if we are hospitalized for cardiac arrest or at home in bed, again, with a migraine. To keep the human body running in tip-top condition, I recommend scheduling some "me time" at regular intervals. A woman's last nerve is fragile and highly flammable. Do not let your family or your job get anywhere near it. Besides taking mental health vacations, it's also important to practice *selective* amnesia and alter your daily routine with a pinch of variety.

AVOID EMOTIONAL MISCARRIAGES

The human body is a remarkable machine. It can survive for weeks on water alone. It can heal broken hearts without antibiotics and, during a crisis, keep functioning with no food for weeks! But why test your body's limits? The machine works and lasts longer if you give it nutritious food, proper medical care, exercise, and—the most important fuel of all—rest.

*Don't ignore the yellow lights on the
dashboard of your life.*

It is a well-documented fact that bodies subjected to chronic, long-term stress become weak and are susceptible to disease. Some symptoms of poor physical and emotional health are very obvious, like chest pain or panic attacks. Other symptoms are often ignored or attributed to "female issues," with hormonal fluctuations being among the favorite suspects. Remember, your body, like your car, usually warns you before it breaks down completely. It's important to notice the yellow lights on the dashboard of your life.

Subtle signs of pending physical or emotional illness include:

✓ insomnia

✓ hair loss

✓ lack of energy

✓ irritability with everything and everyone

✓ feelings of hopelessness

✓ body aches unrelated to activity

✓ constant worry (anxiety)

✓ skin rashes

✓ suicidal thoughts

✓ loss of interest in your social life

✓ hallucinations

✓ loss of interest in sex (assuming you were interested before)

✓ eating too much or too little

✓ excessive drinking of alcoholic beverages

✓ difficulty concentrating

Short-term depression of a few weeks or months, particularly following the loss of a loved one or job, is normal. However, if these symptoms persist, begin to interfere with your relationships, and decrease the quality of your life, then you need more than jogging and Pilates.

Visit www.mayoclinic.com and read the article on "Generalized Anxiety Disorder" for helpful information. Remember, your mental health is intimately related to your physical health.

It is critical to change your lifestyle *and* consult a health care professional when you begin to suffer from the *spiritual anorexia* that usually precedes self-destruction. Yes, women self-destruct. We plant landmines in our minds every time someone hurts us. During those unplanned trips down memory lane, we sometimes forget where we buried the bombs. You don't have to live life so dangerously. In the words of someone smarter than me, "Don't go there."

Where should you go? Try these rejuvenating activities:

1. **Go to bed** and sleep seven to eight hours even if you need a prescribed sleep aid for a short term. Your insomnia may be related to negative changes in your body chemistry. Your physician should advise you in this area. Your body repairs and rejuvenates while you sleep. If you're not getting enough rest, you are really asking for trouble. If you're the type to lose track of time, put bedtime in your smart phone. Set the alarm. When it goes off, stop what you're doing and go nighty-night, like a third grader. Not many third graders have high stress–related blood pressure.

2. **Go on vacation.** Plan it in advance. Try to take at least two a year: one with the girls and one with your family. If that's not an option, as discussed earlier, go alone. A whopping 30 percent of employees forego their vacation days. That hasn't prevented one person from being downsized. You are dispensable. If we can replace the president of the United States, you can be replaced also. Some major employers now require their employees to take their vacations because rested employees tend to be healthier and more creative. Ever notice how you're

bursting with ideas after a vacation or a good night's sleep? That's no coincidence. That's a resuscitated mind.

3. **Go to the spa** or any place where you can get a little pampering. If you can afford it (especially with a coupon), do the whole spa day, including lunch. If not, get a spa pedicure for less than the cost of a skinny cocktail and nice meal. Don't take your tablet. Don't check your e-mail or update your status. Breathe in the lavender scents, listen to the waterfall and soothing music, or do nothing for one hour. Consider it a mini-vacation.

4. **Go out!** Leave the house. Leave the television. Leave the Internet. If you don't have friends, make some. Go to www.meetup.com, put in your zip code and interest, and locate a group of fun people in your area who share your leisure activity interest. If you have friends, spend time with them. Texting and e-mail forwards do not constitute a relationship. Is your money funny? Have a potluck and watch DVDs at someone's home. Go outside and look at the stars or watch the clouds float by. The view is awesome! Occasionally, shift your focus from collecting material things to collecting memories. When you breathe your last breath, memories are all you take away, and that's really all you leave behind.

....
Don't take better care of your Buick than your body.
....

Successful women, those who dance the Career Calypso and survive to the next round, are the ones who strive for a balanced life that includes work and play. Too much of either is detrimental to our health. Like overstimulated children, occasionally we need a time-out. Our bodies demand it. If we don't schedule it ourselves, our bodies take the initiative in the form of a respiratory infection, mysterious fever, fatigue, or some other ailment with no known origin. Don't take better care of your Buick than your body. If you're running on empty, it's time for a rest stop.

PRACTICE SELECTIVE AMNESIA

The news media is on an unending quest to bring the public what I call "WTF?" stories. Uniformly lacking newsworthiness, but extremely high on the peculiar behavior meter, the stories are quickly forgotten, replaced by the newest weird thing. One such story introduced America to people who never forget anything. They remember, with perfect recall, important events that happened on a randomly selected day, even if the day was twenty years ago. These people can tell you what they ate, wore, and did on the sixteenth day of school back in the third grade. In some ways, this gift of a perfect memory is a blessing. Imagine never forgetting special occasions. If you remembered the exact day that a friend's ex-husband married his mistress, you could plan a little something—maybe a party celebrating your friend's svelte Divorce Diet figure—to brighten her day. Never forgetting the birthday of an elderly neighbor would be a deposit in your good deeds account. And can you imagine never forgetting what you entered a room to do or where you placed your car keys?

Remembering everything might seem like a gift, but I respectfully decline. Why? Occasionally, a little selective amnesia is a lifesaver. The truism "time heals all wounds" is rooted in the notion of forgetfulness as a way of moving from a bad place in the past to a better place in the future. From the child who cries while getting an immunization shot one minute and smiles over a lollipop the next, to the widow who, two years after her partner's death, can think of him with a painless smile, every person can experience the healing benefits of deleting some of his or her past.

*Deliberately blanking out negative events
will positively change your life.*

Forgetting (or amnesia, if you will) and the healing that follows occur naturally, if we let them. If you have something in your life that you can't get over, chances are that you engage in behavior that gets in the way of nature's plans. If you are really trying to forget your ex's phone number, delete it from your phone! In the rare circumstance that you need to reach him later, you can most likely do so through his job or mutual acquaintances. Learning to allow time to carry you to the next level, to stop immersing yourself in a situation or person who is best forgotten, takes a lot of practice, but the more you do it, the better you become at letting it be.

I understand that some things cannot be forgotten easily because they were (or worse case scenario, still are) thrust at us regularly. Take a person who, as a child, was repeatedly told she's stupid and ugly. Or what about the sterling employee who is unfairly passed over for promotion year after year? Who can voluntarily forget things like that?

You can't do it easily, but you can deliberately delete events, destructive criticism, and even people who are unforgettably awful in a way that allows you to move forward with your life. The first step in practicing selective amnesia is to separate the things you need to remember from those that you should forget. This might be the toughest part of the exercise, because it requires you to be honest with yourself, about yourself. Imagine that during an argument, your spouse or teenager accuses you of being overbearing. You shouldn't automatically put all that criticism in the selective amnesia bin. Honestly assess whether you are sometimes bossy or always have to have the last word. Entertain the idea that the comment might be 100 percent true. Don't lie. If the comment is 30 percent true and 70 percent jackazz, you still have room for improvement. Determine when your insistence that things go your way is just plain petty. Make a plan for self-improvement, relax, and acknowledge that other people need to make their own decisions and their own mistakes. You cannot (nor do you want to) be in charge of the entire world. That position has been filled.

That takes care of the 30 percent—what about the rest of it? Maybe your teenage daughter really piled it on thick, telling you no one likes you because you are such a know-it-all. Has anyone else said this about you? If an honest, brutal inventory of your habits and a frank conversation with an honest friend reveals that your grounded child's comment is simply part of the hurt-people-hurt-people syndrome, it's time for selective amnesia.

Examples from the workplace might include that bad presentation you gave at the last staff meeting or the client who demanded a new rep because you failed to satisfy his or her outrageous demands. Do you quit your job in order to avoid the possible humiliation of a recurrence? Of course not! You try again. You learn what you can from the experience to improve your future efforts and go for it. Failure is only habit forming if you intentionally repeat it again and again. And that's what you're doing when you replay a bad experience in your head night after night. Let it go. Replace that nightmare with a vision of success.

....

Put nonproductive to-dos on your to-don't list!

....

Sounds good, but how do you do it? Here is a good technique for transporting emotional baggage. Put the things you choose to remember before you. Yes, *before,* like "in front of." Imagine your complete history of flops in a grocery cart, uncovered in all their painful glory. Now what? First, stop crying. Then, discard the spoiled, leftover emotions and keep the great lessons learned. Now, you have two options:

1. Pull them behind you.

2. Push them in front of you.

Pulling failure is awkward and painful, and it slows you down way too much. If this were an effective way of transporting things, we'd use it for grocery shopping. Pushing your mistakes in front of you is much more efficient. At a glance, you see what's in the pile.

Just g-l-a-n-c-e, folks. Don't stare at your failures any longer than you stare at your groceries. See what you need to see and check out of the past.

When you encounter a situation similar to one from your past, look at those life lessons and avoid doing the same unproductive thing. Same action gets the same results. Duh. If you fail at trying something new, quickly put it in the stack and keep moving. Be sure to notice if you have several of the same items in the collection, such as the same dead-end job, dead-end relationship, or dead-end argument. Inevitably, the pile will grow, but it should grow from new errors made during new efforts, not with twenty pink slips because you can't get your night-owl, channel-surfing, snooze-button-slamming self to work on time every morning. The lesson there is: you need a night job, Honey Boo Boo!

Keep trying! You are not too old, too young, or too dumb. Learn your lesson and graduate, girlfriend. The saddest women on earth are the ones with no dreams.

Selective amnesia will help rid you of the mental and physical clutter slowing you down and preventing you from attaining your goals. Choosing to forget gives you a clean slate on which to write your own story, happy ending and all.

TAKE THE SCENIC ROUTE HOME

Have you ever known a person whose freedom is restricted? Look in the mirror, because we all have our freedom restricted to some degree—we are not able to do whatever we want, whenever we want. Try walking outside to the mailbox in the nude tomorrow if you don't believe that's true. A restriction isn't always imposed upon us. It can be temporary and voluntary. Curtailing your social life to save money or spending more time with family are good examples. Or, the restriction on freedom might be an inevitable stage of life—limitations brought on by disease or age, for example.

For most of us, changing the way we live is not a life-or-death decision. We float through our daily routines, content as long as things are pretty much okay. We women are better than anyone at filling our time with dutiful tasks that end up making one day look like the next. Rather than roll through life like five-time Wimbledon Champion, Venus Williams, taking on new challenges in new places year after year, we pedal around like a skeptical two-year-old on a tricycle, tracing and retracing the same circular path on an unyielding concrete sidewalk. Just like that two-year-old who cannot leave the driveway, we may begin a routine because we do not have much of a choice: the kids must be off to school by six in the morning, we must be at the office by seven, dinner must be served precisely eleven hours later, only to start over again the next day. Before long, we have created a very deep rut.

When circumstances change, the children get older and become more self-sufficient, for example, we stay in the rut, not because we enjoy it, but because we don't know how to climb out of the comfortable hole we've dug for ourselves.

Remove the dust from your dreams so you can see them more clearly.

If your life amounts to a case study in repetition accompanied by a long "if I had the time" wish list, maybe it's time you rev up your routine and take the scenic route to personal fulfillment.

How do you know if you are in a rut? There are telltale signs… like the amount of time you spend surfing the computer or watching television. If you can recite from memory the Monday through Friday sitcom lineup, you are in a rut. If you eat the same foods week after week, see the same people, and instinctively say "no" when invited to do something new, it is time for a change. If you have sex on the same two nights a week, every week, for the same period of time, foreplay optional, you are in a rut. It is invigorating to be unpredictable at times. People who do the same thing, the same way, every day are usually boring. Journalist Katie Couric and Supreme Court Justice Sonia Sotomayor are living proof that being reliable is not the same as being boring. Think about it. Don't most of us prefer movies with a happy, but surprising ending or books with plot twists and multifaceted characters?

The first step to changing one's habits is also the hardest one—changing one's mind. Once we are programmed to think a certain way, and to ignore the possibilities that exist outside that world, it becomes hard to change course. So many women who were party animals in their twenties go into complete hibernation by their mid- to late thirties. Invite them out on a Saturday night for a play or concert, and all you get is excuses about how tired they are and how busy they are, as if the rest of us have easy jobs where we sleep all day. Yep. I'm tired, too, sometimes but not *every* weekend! C'mon. Live a little.

....

The only constant is change, continuing
change, inevitable change; that is the dominant
factor in society today. ~ Isaac Asimov

....

Consider those workaholics with weeks of vacation time who refuse to take a day off to explore their own city or visit another. Ask why, and the answer might be, "It's too much trouble." No, mopping your kitchen floor every day is too much trouble. No one is ever going to eat off of it.

Take action. Start small; do something simple, yet different, from anything you've done before. How about your drive home from work? The rational route home is the one that is quickest and safest, and that is the one you likely take. You probably pass neighborhoods or unusual stores that make you think, "hmmm, that looks interesting." Yet you never park and stroll around because doing so would change your normal route and use up valuable gasoline.

To start your journey away from the mundane, the next time you feel the impulse to go someplace new, act on it immediately. Don't wait, postpone, or debate with yourself. If you don't act within ten seconds, it's unlikely you will do it. Spontaneity is okay when it allows you to be an intellectual tourist in the city you inhabit every day.

Shift into discovery mode and explore with childlike wonder. You'll feel a spark of excitement at having done something different. Look, feel, smell, and listen to everything around you. Perhaps you'll discover a little boutique or café you weren't aware of before.

Check out the park with the duck pond or that independent book-store. I guarantee there are parts of your city that are like little treasures waiting to be discovered by you.

Changing your schedule in this way might add thirty minutes to your commute or maybe an hour to your Saturday morning walks, depending on how adventurous you are. Either way, taking the scenic route is an easy way to bring the color back into a black-and-white lifestyle.

*The first step to changing one's habits
is changing one's mind.*

Getting out of a rut is not as hard as you think. Check out this website for activities that you can become involved in *today*: www.PlayDateUs.com. Their motto is "You don't stop playing because you get old, you get old because you stopped playing."

LESSON NINE SUMMARY

☞ Your mind and your body require daily preventive maintenance. Don't take better care of your car than your heart.

☞ Balanced lifestyles include work *and* play.

☞ Practicing "selective amnesia" will help you move beyond difficult experiences.

☞ Don't waste time on nonproductive tasks until income-producing tasks are completed.

☞ Changing your mind is the first step toward changing your habits.

Lesson Ten: Love Yourself First

WE LEARN TO "love thy neighbor as thyself." No wonder there is so much fear, anger, and loathing in the world. Entirely too many of us do not love ourselves. Not as we should. We do not love our bodies because they are not fashion magazine perfect. We do not establish boundaries when others trespass on our emotional and intellectual territory. We are not satisfied in bed or out of it. Well, it is time to live, make love, and laugh as if you are solely responsible for your happiness because, ultimately, you are.

THE COUGAR MYTH

Women in leadership roles invariably evoke debates about feminism and sexuality. I dream of a world where we are not subjected to the assumption that we can be smart or sexy but rarely both. I doubt I will see that mountaintop, but I do believe that it exists.

Take the current fascination with "cougars." Some of my colleagues blanch when they hear the term. I say, if we can't beat it, let's own it and redefine it. The media, fashion magazines, and movies have inexplicably changed the meaning of *cougar* from "big cat" to "aging sex kitten." Is that a compliment or an unfair depiction of experienced, accomplished women who happen to have an unlimited dating pool by default, rather than by design? This tendency to define self-reliant women by their sensuality while discarding their success diminishes them and, by extension, every female who has spent four and more decades morphing from a defenseless kitty into a woman of means. Think about it. How often is someone who is not independent referred to as a cougar? Pretty much never. Right?

Quiet as it is kept, "cougars" are not sexual objects of a certain age who prefer young, virile men. They don't work at being "hot" because manufactured hotness eventually cools. But that never-say-die sexy at sixty or seventy (like Tina Turner) potency is a result of confidence, a healthy lifestyle, independence, and a beautiful spirit that loves, despite the pain that love sometimes brings. It is an irresistible, powerful charisma that exudes through the pores—from the inside out.

....

Self-love is the genesis of sexy.

....

A real cougar is as sexy in a T-shirt and jogging shorts as she is in a Vera Wang gown, simply because she believes she is sexy. You cannot buy cougar sexy in the lingerie department. You cannot spray it on your pulse points or earn it by sleeping with every man you meet. Sexy is not a pose or position; it is a state of mind. It is the movement of one's hand, with unintended grace, when emphasizing a point. It is the flash of lightning in a compassionate woman's eyes when she sees injustice. It's the way one holds a wine glass as if she owns the liquor, the fluted glass, and the vineyard. This species of cougar is not ashamed of who they are or how they are; they love their close-enough-to-perfect selves. Self-love imparts a certain *je ne sais quoi* or inexpressible quality that cannot be captured nor killed.

Moreover, authentic cougars are not man-eaters any more than cougars in the wild because they truly enjoy expressing their love. They mate for life. For some, "life" means *life force* and for others it means *forever*. The ultimate, but elusive, soul mate alliance combines the two objectives. If you find that, never, never, never let it go.

ANGELINA JOLIE IS NOT A SEX SYMBOL

These are the facts about her double mastectomy as relayed by Angelina Jolie. Her mother died of ovarian cancer after a decade-long struggle; she was in her midfifties. With that very bad news in her medical history, Jolie made the wise decision to have genetic testing and learned the odds of her suffering a similar fate are very high. Jolie wrote a moving op-ed piece about the difficult decision to have a double mastectomy in the *New York Times*. "My doctors estimated that I had an 87 percent risk of breast cancer and a 50 percent risk of ovarian cancer, although the risk is different in the case of each woman."

Jolie is a beautiful woman. She is a daughter, mother, partner, actress, and outspoken activist. She is mortal and, therefore, made a decision that she hopes will extend her relative immortality. I know it seems drastic to remove both breasts when you don't actually have cancer. Look at it this way. If there was an 87 percent chance that you might be killed if you set one foot outside your home tomorrow, would you leave the house? What if it was your parents' fiftieth wedding anniversary and your only child's first day of school and the absolute only day you could pick up your lottery winnings of one million dollars—would you take that chance? I don't think I would, but I really can't say because I don't have to make a decision quite that difficult when I get up in the morning.

What I do know is that my physical appearance would not be a factor in my deliberations, and shame on all the people who seem more concerned with the change in her breasts than the change in her life. That doesn't just objectify her; it objectifies all women. You've seen her movies. You've seen her rainbow tribe of children. And, of course, you've seen her red carpet photo shots with partner, Brad Pitt. Today, you see another side of Angelina Jolie. Call it what you want, but don't use the term "sex symbol." She is much more than that.

She's a symbol of strength.

PRACTICE PASSION

In the final analysis, whether you consider yourself a cougar or a countess, you set your own goals for your love life. Simply remember that a relationship is work, not a vacation from life. That includes what goes on in the bedroom. The ten o'clock news does not signal quitting time. If you want to keep the home fires burning, do like the early settlers and stoke the fire: add fuel to keep the flames flickering, or the fire will burn out.

You don't have to be the next woman to lapse into a coma from an overdose of the missionary position. Face it. If you've been together for years, you've seen all his moves. He probably doesn't know any more positions. If he does, he's afraid to use them because you'll wonder where he learned them. You can learn together. There are DVDs, books, and dozens of aids to help you.

Think of your love life as a job you actually like. If sales or employee morale drops, you think of new strategies. Right? Likewise, if his interest in you wanes or you begin to find him as boring as shopping for socks online, be proactive and make some changes. Keep things exciting for both of you. Take the lead in bringing freshness to a stagnant relationship, and he will follow suit.

Sex is not everything. Chocolate is everything, but research has shown that a healthy sex life does result in a longer life expectancy, better sleep, and a higher level of happiness. (So does chocolate, but that is not the point.) The lesson is that the happiest women know a great sex life, as part of a well-balanced life, takes effort, ingenuity, and teamwork, just like everything else we want to accomplish. Great sex is a goal, not a given. If you want an amazing sex life, don't expect it to happen like magic. Make a plan and take action. Act as if you are responsible for arranging the arrival of your ecstasy. Approach it like a project manager. Now, what will you do differently?

*The stock market may rise and fall,
but investing in your love life always
pays dividends.*

LOVE, LAUGH, AND LIVE
(BENEFITS OF HUMOR)

We know laughter is good for the soul. Researchers at many prestigious institutions have done studies demonstrating a clear correlation between our attitudes and our well-being. There is a good reason we enjoy being around positive people and watching sitcoms. Laughing literally makes us feel better. It has numerous benefits... from lowering the blood pressure to exercising our abdominal muscles to boosting our immune system. Happy people heal faster. Plus, laughter, unlike most prescription medicine, has no negative side effects, no co-pay, no waiting period, and no deductible.

If we measure success by the number of times you smile genuinely or laugh heartily every pay period, what would your income be? It's a fact; happiness is becoming underrated, almost disdained by some people as a frivolous, nonprofit pursuit. My grandmother Lucile, mother of fifteen, had a dry wit that often left me in stitches even as an adult. Once, I was lamenting to my grandma about a series of mishaps that felt like persecution from the universe. I said, "I think God is picking on me." Without missing a beat, she replied, "Do tell. I didn't think God had that much free time." The absurdity of my statement became immediately apparent, and all I could do was laugh along with her.

There is an advantage to taking the road less traveled. In an increasingly stressful world, it is easy to take popular routes like hopelessness or selfishness. Others become drama queens and drama kings. Screaming never makes a bad situation better. When you find yourself yelling at everyone about every-little-thing, it's time to stop and count your blessings. Yes, Interstate Nasty Attitude has many lanes, but after a while, the tolls add up and the emotional price becomes too high.

Some women act as if nothing bothers them. They never cry, never sweat, never seem depressed...*never*. Nah, don't believe 'em. Even saints have bad days. Those stoic folks are probably on prescription drugs. Seriously, hundreds of millions of Americans are on antihypertensives for their stress-related high blood pressure, antidepressants for their mood swings, and antianxiety drugs for their last nerve. Of course, I believe in prescription medication. I've seen medicine help the body heal infections in countless patients. But unless your psychological issues are organic or genetic, prescription medication should not be like vitamins you plan to take every day for the rest of your life. No, at some point, we need to learn other ways to deal with the adversity in our lives.

Rose-colored glasses are never made in bifocals:
nobody wants to read the small print in dreams.
~ Ann Landers

The women who are the healthiest and have the most spiritual wealth have multiple sources of happiness: family, work, hobbies, community involvement, a sense of adventure, and the ability to find humor in even the direst situation. Life is too precious to worry yourself to death. Scientists at numerous prestigious institutions have presented research suggesting that laughter may be a buffer against disease.

Here are a few of the medical benefits of laughter:

* relaxes the body while simultaneously exercising stomach and facial muscles

* reduces blood pressure and heart rate

* releases endorphins, the body's natural painkiller

* improves circulation and breathing, providing more oxygen to the body. With more blood to the brain, you think better and your memory improves.

* boosts the immune system, in order for your body to better fight infection

Humor and optimism are indispensable. Today, begin managing your happiness as deliberately as you manage your business affairs. Develop a plan for living happily before a chronically negative, pessimistic attitude consumes your soul. Change will come. Actively seek it instead of passively awaiting the results of chaos. You do have a choice.

Norman Cousins, the longtime editor of the *Saturday Review*, is known as the man who laughed his way to good health. In the 1960s, he was diagnosed with a life-threatening collagen disease that slowly paralyzes the body. His physicians told him that his death was inevitable. Cousins refused to accept the bad prognosis. He refused to let the limits of science and medicine become the limits of his faith. Against the advice of his doctors, Cousins left the hospital. With the help of friends and family, he started a radical new therapy that he designed himself. It included a nutritional program with high doses of vitamin C, and equally important, it included even higher doses of humor. He watched funny programs like the Marx Brothers and *Candid Camera*. A nurse read him funny stories every day. He did anything he could to make himself laugh. We now refer to this as "humor therapy."

And we all feel better after a good laugh don't we? That's why comedic films and sitcoms continue to top the Nielsen ratings for viewership in every demographic.

In time, Cousins got better. He said the genuine laughter relieved his pain. Slowly but surely, he regained the use of his limbs. Eventually, he returned to work full-time. In 1979, he wrote *Anatomy of an Illness*, a best-selling book about his experience. He credited his recovery from that disease—and years later, his recovery from a massive heart attack—to his healthy diet plus his optimistic attitude.

Most certainly, I am not suggesting that anyone ever stop using a prescription medication or go against a physician's advice. However, I am convinced that a positive outlook is beneficial to our health.

Certainly, there are challenges in every life. Before you can see the silver lining, there's usually a dark cloud. The Bible refers to these challenges as "seasons" in the book of Ecclesiastes. These seasons include not only "a time to weep" but also, "a time to laugh… and a time to dance…"

Sometimes obstacles come in the form of the people around you, and sometimes they come from perfect strangers who seem intent on making your life a nightmare.

For example, I made a simple phone call the other day. As usual, I was placed on hold immediately by an automated voice that said,

"Thank you, for your patience. Someone from customer service will be with you before the next millennium."

An hour later, I was thinking, "I can't hang up. I've invested too much time into this call. If I hang up, I'll lose my place in the infinitely long line of people waiting to speak to a human being, any human being, at this company." Thank goodness for mobile phones. I was able to purchase groceries, fill my car up with gas, cook a four-course meal and clean up the kitchen while waiting for a customer service representative.

It all started innocently enough. While reviewing my credit card statement, I found an item that I had a question about. A simple question. So I dialed the toll-free service number under the illusion that I could resolve the matter in a few minutes. Instead, I got this:

"Thank you for calling Bank of Eternity. For faster service, please have your account number available."

Okay, got it right here. No problem.

"For account information or service, press one. To apply for a new account, press two. To hear an oral reading of volumes one and two of the *Encyclopedia Britannica* while you wait, press three."

Well, that's a nice attempt at humor, I thought. Little did I realize—they were serious. So I pressed one.

Then I heard, "Please enter your twenty-digit account number followed by the pound key within the next ten seconds."

It took me five attempts to accomplish that feat within the time limit. I was disconnected twice in the meantime. After that, I received more instructions.

"Please enter the last two digits of your mother's weight on her eighteenth birthday, followed by the pound key."

I clicked over, called my mom, verified the information, hung up with mom, and entered the two digits. I kept thinking that at any moment they were going to ask me to slay a dragon to prove that I actually deserved to speak to a customer service representative.

Finally, there appeared a light at the end of the tunnel when I heard the automated voice say, "Please hold while we connect you to your account representative."

Two days later, I finally heard a real voice.

"Thank you for waiting. This is Tammy. May I have your account number, please?"

"But Tammy, I just entered my account number five times. Didn't your computer save it or something?"

Tammy sighed. "Well, ma'am, our computers have been down most of the day, so that information didn't transfer. May I please have your account number, your telephone number, and your home address?"

"But Tammy, when I applied for the card. I gave a deposition on everything there is to know about me. I even sent you a vial of blood with the fourteen certified copies of my birth certificate. Isn't that account number linked to my account information?"

"Ma'am, I just work here. There are two of us left since they downsized the department. We share a single computer and it's ten years old. Jean takes care of twenty-five states and I handle the others. I'm sure all of your information is in the computer somewhere, but I could carve it in stone faster than I can pull it up."

Fine. I gave her all of my information again and waited some more while she went to lunch. When she came back from lunch, she asked me, "What was your question, ma'am?"

By now, I could hardly remember my question.

"Well, there's a seven-cent charge on my card for some kind of phone or Internet service. I've never heard of this company. Can you tell me anything about these charges?"

"Ma'am, you'll have to call the company for that information."

"What company is it? All I have here are some initials."

"I understand ma'am. I'd like to help you but unfortunately, I just noticed that you live in Texas."

"And?"

"Ma'am, that's Jean's area. I'll have to transfer you. Please hold."

DON'T TELL HIM YOUR PLANS

O'Veria Clinton lay in her claw-footed bed, advanced in wisdom and allergic to social grace. Though beloved by her friends and family, their visits with her were hurried, and made out of duty, not desire. Her mind seemed to aimlessly bounce from decade to decade, recounting events while everybody repeatedly glanced at their cell phones, hoping they would ring.

Then one Sunday evening O'Veria dropped a verbal bomb. She stared at her visitors, two ladies who were newer to the world than the quilt on O'Veria's bed, and said, "Don't ever tell a man what you're gonna do—just do it." She added that threatening to leave a relationship when someone mistreats you is a waste of time and breath. Her rule was simple, "Don't keep telling him you're going to leave. Girls, leave!"

....

Don't ever tell a man what you're
going to do—just do it.

....

The women scooted to the edge of their chairs like little girls on their first day of music lessons. They remembered O'Veria's husband, their great-uncle, who was handsome, kind, and a fun companion. Being married and having a partner who fully commits "'til death do us part" (about sixty years in O'Veria's case) was an abstract concept to them. *How did she do it*, they wanted to know. O'Veria replied that her methodology was simple.

She said to keep peace in her home she kept him fed, made him feel respected, and she didn't ever allow boredom into the bedroom. She said it much more graphically, but you get the picture. Lastly, she advised, when problems do arise, you must know how to draw the line. On one side of the line are words, on the other side, action.

Many of us have difficulty embracing the simple concept that, sometimes, actions are the only answer. Our impulse is to talk and overanalyze. Why won't he commit to the relationship? (The same reason he didn't commit to his last two girlfriends.) Why did he blow a hole in our savings account? (Again? He does it every hunting season, remember?) Why does he put his friends' needs before mine? (He was doing that before you moved in. Hello?)

In 1920, George Santayana wrote an essay titled "What People Will Put Up With." The following delicious sentence always stuck with me. "Habit is stronger than reason, and the respect for fact stronger than the respect for the ideal." Wow! *Habit is stronger than reason.* So despite the best intentions, we revert to old habits unless we consciously force ourselves to act in new ways until they become habitual.

If someone in a relationship injures you emotionally or physically over and over, it doesn't matter how badly the person feels about it, nor does it matter that he or she recognizes the problem. Talking will not change his or her destructive habit. That's why the nagging and late night lectures are not working. Both of you must take action to bring about change.

We all know well-meaning parents who yell and threaten but never does anything, so their children continue to misbehave. If a three-year-old recognizes an idle threat, you can be sure a thirty-year-old does, as well.

What keeps us talking rather than acting? It's learned behavior. Standing your ground could lead to a big argument, and who knows what might happen? You might get called an ugly name, right? Or, if we press too hard, our lover might leave, and we'll be all alone again. So, we keep talking in circles and getting the same unsatisfying result.

··

Don't make excuses; make changes.

··

Which brings us back to ol' O'Veria's line in the sand. The ability to love herself, her truth, and her right to be treated with dignity, gave her the strength to act. She thought of herself as a beautiful, desirable woman, and if her husband failed to appreciate her, she believed someone else would. Uncle Clinton knew she loved him and she didn't want to leave. In fact, it would be her last resort, but, if necessary, she was not afraid to change her life—and his Compare the following statements:

A. I'm going to tell him our six-year engagement is off, and I bet he will finally set a wedding date.

B. I'm giving the ring back and breaking our six-year engagement tonight. Whatever happens happens.

Statement A is a threat and an attempt at manipulation. Statement B is taking charge of your future and being willing to accept the consequences.

Sometimes we must love from a distance rather than be destroyed up close.

Let me be clear, I hate ending committed relationships. No one should ever come to that point in his or her relationship. I know firsthand the devastating impact of terminating a marriage. Part of the healing process for me was spending a lot of time understanding the role I played in what happened. Because really the only person we can change is ourselves. Right?

If you haven't read the book *The 5 Love Languages* by Gary Chapman, now is the time. It is my favorite go-to for understanding how to express my needs in all of my relationships, meaning with family, friends, or whomever. Chapman gives great advice and specific language for getting things back on track.

So what if you've tried everything and nothing seems to work? When you love someone, it's hard to let go even when you know you should. If the person genuinely loves you back, there is always a chance for forgiveness and reconciliation later, on terms that are mutually beneficial. Until then, you may have to love him or her at arm's length. This may be the hardest challenge, but that action, loving from a distance rather than being destroyed up-close, might be the only way to save yourself from spiritual or physical death. Action is strong medicine, for sure, and as with any powerful tonic, if it does not kill your relationship, it just might make it healthier.

LESSON TEN SUMMARY

☞ Authentic cougars are sexy from the inside out.

☞ A great sex life takes effort, ingenuity, and teamwork.

☞ Humor benefits your body mentally and physically.

☞ Don't give ultimatums. Actions speak louder than words.

☞ Always attack the problem, not the person.

☞ Be prepared for a positive *or* negative reaction to your action.

☞ Love from a distance if the alternative is being destroyed up-close.

Lesson Eleven:
Multiple Streams of Happiness

A GOOD FINANCIAL portfolio has multiple streams of income, and a well-balanced life has multiple streams of happiness. Happiness is the antidote to chaos. Happiness is to emotional well-being what exercise is to physical health. You should always schedule time for family, hobbies, volunteering, and other personal interests. When your self-worth is super glued to a single phase of your life, you risk losing every ounce of joy if something unexpected, like a job loss, occurs. Deposit your past successes, future hopes, and present opportunities to help others into your happiness account, and you'll never be spiritually bankrupt.

PURSUE YOUR PASSIONS

An essential fundamental for balanced living is to remember your passions, those things you loved to do before you got so busy with your life of details. Do you enjoy making melodious music? Dig that clarinet out of the attic and take lessons. Love dancing? Move the furniture in the family room, turn up the volume, and dance like the stars every Friday night from seven until eight. Have your kid flip the lights on and off and pretend you're at a disco. Consider taking a class. Yeah, yeah, I know. You don't want to go back to school, but this isn't a long-term commitment; it's a single class, not a full schedule. It's a class you choose, on a subject you like, on a day or night that fits *your* schedule. It's a chance to meet new people, stimulate dormant areas of your amazing mind.

Commit to your favorite activity by placing it on your calendar in ALL CAPS so it pops up every time you consult your schedule. You do put important things in your schedule, don't you? Well, your sanity is important. Don't let anything interfere with your plans. I challenge you to spend six measly hours a week on mental fitness. That's 1.8 percent of thirty days or six episodes of *Scandal.* And if you're passionate about television, you may need to spend some non-HDTV time with your partner. Whatever happened to date night, anyway? Why should anything or anyone else be more important than the person who brings you juice when you're sick?

On the other hand, those family matters, especially children, seem to be our favorite excuse for why we don't properly feed our souls. It is hard to find the neutral ground between giving too much to them and taking too much from ourselves. Warning: I am not suggesting pursuing your personal interests to the exclusion of your family. Rather, do it for the benefit of yourself and your family. It should be acceptable for you to spend 1.8 percent of your time at a play or a rock-climbing venue of your choosing. When you reach 25, 30, or 40 percent, be prepared to hear some legitimate, vehement complaints unless you're being paid to do it, in which case it is a job, not a hobby.

THE WALKERS

Avis and T. D. Walker, a "perfect" power couple consisting of two physicians with two young children and an elderly dog, wound up in marriage counseling because of tennis. Yes, tennis…like Venus and Serena at Wimbledon. This devoted mom and dad worked long hours every week, but after leaving corporate America, Avis clocked in on her second job, "domestic goddess" and T. D. grabbed his gear and headed to the lighted tennis courts. He played several evenings a week and all day on Saturday. He attended church with the family on Sunday, and did yard work on Sunday afternoon. Now, imagine what Avis was doing with two kids and a household to manage. This is a formula for disaster.

Avis resented her lack of personal time, and T. D. felt he'd earned the right to unwind and get his exercise on because he "worked hard." Years passed before T. D. came home one night, dumped his sweaty T-shirt in the laundry room for the Washing Fairy to handle, and poured himself a glass of juice. The house seemed more quiet than usual. He assumed the kids were sleeping and his adoring wife must be in the master bedroom preparing for her true love's arrival. He was half-right. The kids were sleep, but fed-up Avis was on a plane headed to San Diego. Why San Diego? She never explained that part. Whatever took her to San Diego kept her there three weeks. She sent no communication to T. D., except for a terse text in all lowercase letters with strange punctuation explaining, "im gone. im fine. might not come back?!"

Aftermath: T. D. now helps around the house, plays tennis only twice a week—doubles with his wife and another couple—and the entire family spends Saturdays together. Still, one wonders what really happened in San Diego.

**

When we neglect ourselves, the people around us also suffer. Your life, your welfare, your happiness should not be an afterthought. It should not be the last thing on your list, even if it is the last thing on everyone else's list. It should be a daily goal. Delegating responsibility to others is not selfishness; it is self-preservation. You are no good to anyone when you're exhausted and irritable.

If we want our children, our younger sisters and brothers, and our friends to have balanced lives that include work, rest, *and* play, we need to role-model balanced lives. We must stop trying to be all things for all people. One of my exes gave me a vacuum cleaner for a gift once because he thought I enjoyed cleaning the house. He said, "You always hum as you dust." Really? Puhleeeeze. I truly like having a clean house, but I'm not particular about how it gets that way. Actually, I was humming "I Will Always Love You." That was Whitney Houston's chart-topping song about leaving her man.

....
Happiness is the antidote to chaos.
....

Speaking of taking people for granted, I enjoyed the movie *The Pursuit of Happyness,* but I wondered why the main character suddenly became so industrious after his wife left. When she was working like one of Pharaoh's slaves, all he did was unsuccessfully sell medical equipment, despite the dire financial predicament of his family. He seemed very unsympathetic to her exhaustion, which stemmed from trying to support a family of three on minimum wage. After she left, he managed to take care of his son, go to class, and successfully sell medical equipment. Yes, he was homeless for a time, and he struggled to balance all the responsibility, but what might have happened if he'd worked that hard before she left? Hmmmmm? Anyway, you alone have the right to decide the direction of your life. If you cannot convince your partner to cooperate and coordinate, there's always San Diego.

Don't sell your soul to the office; they'll never pay you what it's worth.

LEARN HER-STORY

Q. What do the modern dishwasher, the Snugli® baby Carrier, Liquid Paper®, Scotchgard™, and chocolate chip cookies have in common?

A. All were invented by women.

**

An oft-neglected source of motivation is women's history. Despite the numerous mandatory hours of classroom instruction in social studies and history, most of us can only name a few of the legions of females who have irreversibly shaped world history. If we know their names, we generally don't know much of the story behind those names. Knowing their stories can give you a boost when your confidence collapses, as it surely will. This happens to all of us occasionally. When you reach a ceiling, wall, or mountain that seems impenetrable, go back and read the inspiring tales of the amazing women who have overcome worse obstacles than yours with fewer resources. Then, look around you at the contemporary sister soldiers fighting similar domestic battles while refusing to give up.

Yes, history—or rather, "her-story"—can be constructive, building you up, just as it has been destructive, used to viciously destroy women's self-esteem with reminders that "Your mother was a whore" or illogical statements such as "We've never had a female president for a reason." What reason? Women couldn't vote? Women have not had the complete support of a major party?

Did you learn this in history class? Marie Curie was a Nobel Laureate in physics in 1903. "Lady Edison," aka Beulah Louise Henry of Tennessee, was awarded more than one hundred patents! No, you probably didn't hear about these women in history class. In fact, I bet you can count on one hand the number of women you did study in history *and* government.

Take some self-study courses. Visit online resources such as www.About.com and read articles on "Women in History" to learn more about female inventors and female firsts. You won't find these books on any bestseller lists, but they should be. Bear in mind, American women could not own patents prior to the first US Patent Act of 1790. That's two to three decades into the Industrial

Revolution, a time in history when American ingenuity was arguably at its peak. That right was not extended to women in many states until the late 1800s because women in these states could not own property, and to this day, a patent is considered intellectual property. So a large number of inventions and co-inventions are not properly attributed to women. For example, there is evidence that Catherine Littlefield Greene and some slaves (who legally were classified as property) assisted Eli Whitney in the development of the cotton gin. Did you hear two words about that in middle or high school? Probably not. But that was then...

Today, before you go online, make a list of *your* "personal bests." Were you the first in your family to graduate from high school, college, or art school? Then, you are persistent. Did you lose 22.3 lbs in 1999? Then, you do have self-discipline. If you did it before, you can do it again. Have you been in a relationship that lasted longer than your leftovers from the pizza place? Well, three days is a start. Now, shoot for four days with the next guy. You survived chemo and radiation? Wow. That's more amazing than what Sarah Boone achieved as the woman who invented the ironing board. Did you plan a fabulous four-day weekend for you and your girlfriends? Great. You can set goals, organize, coordinate, and manage time, no matter what your boss said on that performance appraisal.

Recognize and appreciate your own successful her-story, in addition to the accomplishments of other great achievers. Your-story is a valuable, irreplaceable patch in the quilt of history. Together, by insisting that women's bold feats receive equal acclaim for equal achievement, we'll make HIS-tory become OUR-story too.

THE GIFT OF FORGIVENESS

A treasured friend recently confided that she is very angry at someone. So angry, in fact, that she has not spoken to the person in months. I didn't understand what she was angry about, but I've had my temperamental moments, so who am I too judge her reaction? I simply asked her if the person knew she upset her. She said, "No, I didn't tell them." I've heard that before. Rather than engage in a conversation that could lead to conflict, we choose to withdraw physically and emotionally. Pent-up anger is similar to an autoimmune disorder, I think. (That instinctive emotion literally changes your body's chemistry and grows into something life threatening when left untreated.)

From the backseat of your life, if I may offer a final word of advice, either let it out or let it go.

Constructively let whomever offended you know that you have an issue with his or her actions/words, or anonymously forgive the person and move on. Keep your distance, if necessary, but let the *mad*ness go. It folks don't know, they *can't* care that they hurt you. Why compound that irony by hurting yourself?

When you hold resentment toward another, you are bound to that person or condition by an emotional link that is stronger than steel. Forgiveness is the only way to dissolve that link and get free.
~ Katherine Ponder

Evangelist T. D. Jakes says it best: some of us need to learn "the art of letting go." Releasing the past is a gift to your future.

**

THE GIST OF IT ALL—MY STORY

Role models for overcoming adversity became even more important to me when I was diagnosed with a rare malignancy known as gastrointestinal stromal tumor (GIST) on February 18, 2011. As I type this chapter, I cannot remember what I am wearing without looking down, but I recall every detail of the day—the date, place, time, and even the way the ER doctor lowered her eyes before informing me: "You have a mass in your abdomen."

I am a wordsmith. I have been writing books, articles, speeches, poems, and songs since I learned to make my mark. Writing is my preferred form of expression, rivaled only by my ability to talk at great lengths about almost anything. (My friends are nodding and smiling here.) Word play and my sense of humor have been my crutches through fifty years of –isms: sexism, regionalism, racism. I'm not complaining. It ism what it ism. Right?

But in that long moment after the diagnosis that changed my life forever, I was totally speechless. I had had a physical the previous month, and everything was fine from my blood work to my mammogram. *How could I have cancer?* I wondered. I was very ill from the food poisoning that had prompted my visit to the Emergency Room, but otherwise, I felt perfectly fine. There I was all alone at four in the morning being confronted with my greatest fear. I had nothing to lean on but my memories of whispered reassurances. After every tumble, my village raised me again, saying, "Get up. You'll be okay. Just get up and try again."

So that's what I did. I endured the brutal surgery to remove the largest tumor, and, with the amazing support of my loved ones, I recovered to my happy new normal.

GIST does not respond to traditional chemotherapy or radiation. As this time, there is no cure. I do oral chemotherapy, a bitter pill, every day and hope they find a cure before the tumors outsmart the pills. The side effects, IVs, and body scans evoke a mile-long stream of four-letter words, but I struggle to find one adjective to describe the actual cancer.

When I was around sixteen years old, three masked robbers came into the fast-food place where I worked. One of them held a gun to my head as he instructed me to put the contents of the cash register into a bag. He didn't say another word. He didn't have to. I knew a worker at another store had been killed in a similar situation, even though she cooperated with their demands. I wondered if I would suffer the same fate. Should I disobey him and fight? Or cooperate and hope for the best? That's what cancer feels like.

Why me? I do not know. And I spend very little time wondering about it.

I now have laser-like focus on the things I am uniquely qualified to do, such as spending a lot more time with my family and friends. Every day I try very hard to do something meaningful that brings me joy—not satisfaction or praise—but measurable happiness. Every day I try to forget the specter of death pressing the barrel of an illegal assault rifle to the back of my head: an unrelenting robber of my time. Most days, I succeed for several hours until fatigue, nausea, or a friendly hug that lasts thirty seconds longer than it did a year ago becomes a whisper from this menace, "Hey you, I'm still here. I may pull this trigger tomorrow or one thousand tomorrows from now. Tick tock, Precious."

That's when I remind myself of all the brave women (and men) who have fought cancer and survived against all odds. That's more history we don't learn in school, like so many of life's greatest lessons.

"I have cancer, but cancer doesn't have me."

I don't know who said it first. I only know that phrase has become my mantra. Each day I rise is a gift from God, not a pardon from death. There are many wonderful people praying for my survival. There are researchers around the world looking for a cure for this very rare cancer. Meanwhile, I take my meds and hope my best achievements help more people than my colossal failures harm. I've decided that I will not pause and wait for death: she will have to catch me. I am a realist by nature. I have planned my funeral down to the words on my tombstone, but I did not die today.

So I shall live—strong.

LESSON ELEVEN SUMMARY

☞ A well-balanced life has multiple streams of happiness.

☞ Pursue your passions.

☞ Spend at least six hours a week on mental fitness.

☞ Become a role model for others seeking a balanced lifestyle.

☞ Use the success stories of people you admire to motivate yourself.

☞ Releasing the past is a gift to your future.

Final Thoughts

THERE IS NO secret recipe to success because it is not a definable destination: a one-size-fits-all place to be or things to own. There is no universal formula like:

Take a cupful of education, a gallon of common sense, two dashes of humor, classic good looks, and a pinch of perseverance. Stir ingredients with a silver spoon, then sift with aggressiveness. Heat in a pressure cooker until you reach the highest tax bracket, but use legal loopholes to avoid actually paying taxes. Cool and serve with a black American Express card.

Yes, all these elements are used by society to judge us, but if the result is still a hollow, lonely feeling, we must change the recipe. We must decide what success looks, sounds, and feels like for us and only us. Striving toward something you actually want makes it easy to wake up smiling. Do you wake up smiling? Do you love the direction of your life? Do you dream during the day? At night? At all? Don't let your fear of the unknown stop you from trying to escape the voluntary misery of an autopilot existence.

You may and you must decide what you need to make you feel strong and happy. When you strive for excellence in achieving those goals—whether for family, a product, a service, or a concept—the side effect is success. Achievement is an experience, not a person, place, or thing.

Decide right now to be brave enough to dream again every day of your life. Work smarter, play harder, and try again. Make Y-O-U a priority on your to-do list. I offer these proven workplace strategies, leadership skills, and personal improvement techniques because I know they work. They will increase your productivity and overall happiness. Trust and believe. It is not too late. Opportunity doesn't expire.

Review. Renew. Re—YOU!

Love & light,
Dr. mOe Anderson, DDS

Acknowledgments

Science fiction authors have the skill and luxury of making things up. My passion is capturing untamed reality, studying it, then re-releasing it to the universe with the best explanation my command of language and life allows.

So, in truth, I owe a big thank-you to everyone I've met because each interaction impacted me and shaped my world view. However, a few have been supportive of my dreams far beyond the boundaries of circumstance. To my beloved, incredible family and dear friends, thank you for the support and sheer kindness of putting up with my intensity. I must acknowledge the amazingly talented and accomplished women who provided constructive feedback and lent me their professional credibility with their endorsements. I am so grateful for my detail-oriented editors, Anita Richmond Bunkley and Kennetta Piper. Big kudos to my longtime photographer, Dwayne Hills, who does amazing artistry with light and lenses. Finally, thank you to Dr. Venus Reese, business coach and inspirational speaker, for writing the foreword and providing a lot of encouragement for this project.

Psalm 118:17: I will not die; instead, [my words] will live to tell what the Lord has done.

Smooches,
mOe

Discussion Questions

1. "Wise and fearless leaders take counsel from everyone." Who is the person you seek counsel from on a consistent basis? What character traits do/should you look for when seeking "wise counsel"?

2. Psychosclerosis is the hardening of your attitude. Identify the areas in your life where you've allowed yourself to become hard or bitter. What is your action plan to soften your approach?

3. Is there a "softer" side of yourself that you need to show? What are the fears associated with revealing your "softer side"?

4. On Maslow's Hierarchy of Needs Pyramid, what unmet needs pose the biggest threat to you becoming your personal best? (Lesson Three)

5. What area(s) in your life have you been avoiding because of fear? Take thirty minutes and devise a plan that moves

you in the direction of addressing/overcoming the fear. (Example: you have a fear of large bodies of water. Plan: sign up for swimming lessons at the YMCA this week.)

6. Take a moment and write down all of the things that you do well (this does not necessarily have to be a strength of yours, but rather something you do well). Create a healthy list of ten to fifteen things. Do all of the things that you do well align into one overall category? Use this list to celebrate yourself and help shape your focus on achieving bigger goals.

7. Successful women consider the flow of traffic in their lives. What risks do you need to take, in spite of the "traffic"? What do you consider the obstacles to be during your travel? (Lesson Four "Analysis Paralysis")

8. What are the main three lessons that you learned from this book? How will you apply these lessons to improve your life?

9. Fear can be paralyzing in our lives. What personal or professional fears have paralyzed you in the past? What is the flip side of that fear? (Lesson Three "Avoid the Fear Factor)

10. What are the expensive material loves of your life? What adjustments do you need to make to help you begin to

save for your future? Not sure? Review last month's bank statement or your Internet search history. In what areas (such as dining out) do you have the most optional expenditures? Do you need to reorder your priorities?

11. Who is on your financial friendship team? (Lesson Six) Who is your financial peer? Your financial superior? What qualities make these people the right members for your financial freedom team?

12. Identify the areas where you must move from the sidelines and onto the playing field. Identify any obstacles that would prevent you from making the transition to being part of the game.

13. In the "Rule Your Queendom" chapter, we were encouraged to "get out, often." Research networking opportunities to attend and *go*! Compare the apprehension you had about attending the event to your actual experience of the event. Do they differ? How?

14. You have probably heard or used the phrase "don't work too hard." Is this actually good advice, or has your thinking changed about it?

15. In what areas of your life do you need to "IN-courage" yourself? What is the action plan to begin doing so? (Lesson Eight)

16. Selective amnesia is deliberately blanking out negative events in order to positively change your life. How can you apply selective amnesia in your life? (Lesson Nine)

17. What does your scenic route to personal fulfillment look like? What things do you visualize on the way?

18. Identify ways that you could change your normal routine to avoid getting stuck in a rut. (Lesson Nine)

19. Think of a time when you attacked a person versus attacking the problem. What was the outcome? What would you do differently?

20. Are there any recurring problems/situations in your life that need to be resolved? The "love yourself first" chapter teaches us that we must draw a line, and on one side are our words and the other side our actions. Take a sheet of paper and draw a vertical line. (The line represents your problem/situation.) On one side of the line, write the words that you associate with that problem/situation, and on the other side of the line write the action(s) that you will employ to change the situation and a concrete deadline to take that action.

About the Author

Monica "Dr. mOe" Anderson is a writer, frequent lecturer, entrepreneur, and licensed doctor of dental surgery. She is currently director of clinical management for a national corporation that administers oral health care programs throughout the United States. She is a former television talk-show host and the author of six books, including the best-selling novel *When a Sistah's Fed Up*. Dr. mOe is an active freelance journalist. Her diverse writing assignments range from movie reviews to dental materials. In 1996, she made history as the first African-American columnist for the *Arlington Star-Telegram*. The popularity of her articles led to a weekly lifestyle column for the *Fort Worth Star-Telegram*, a leading Texas newspaper. Her editorials have appeared in news outlets across the country, as well as Australia. For over two decades, she has given lectures to corporate, university, and civic groups, as well as professional associations across the country. She has also given keynotes internationally encouraging others to maximize their potential. She is the recipient of numerous awards for leadership, community service, and business.

She is a proud mother of two and grandmother. She lives in Texas.

For more:
Visit Monica "Dr. mOe" Anderson's website at
www.drmOeanderson.com
Twitter/@drmOeanderson
iTunes Podcasts/Dr. mOe Anderson
YouTube/drmoeutube

Made in the USA
Charleston, SC
21 March 2015